THE PLEASURE
GROUNDS OF
HOLLAND HOUSE

THE PLEASURE GROUNDS OF HOLLAND HOUSE

BY SALLY MILLER

FOR

THE FRIENDS OF HOLLAND PARK

Front cover. The Summer Ballroom and the ivy-clad arches

CONTENTS

INTRODUCTION

*There is an air of grandeur in it beyond
what the extent should seem to allow.*[1]

ELIZABETH MONTAGUE WROTE THIS after visiting the
park at Holland House in 1765.[2] She was much taken with the
grounds – and impressed by the 'wealth inexhaustible' which had been
spent on laying them out. The owner was Henry Fox (1705–1774), 1st
Baron Holland, and the wealth inexhaustible came from his lucrative post
as Paymaster-General (he appropriated Government funds for his own
use and made more on top by loaning to his friends at high rates of
interest). Elizabeth Montague was a perceptive woman and with this
phrase she identified a key characteristic of the Holland House pleasure
grounds in the mid-eighteenth century: an impression of grandeur in a
relatively modest estate (then 200 acres). This impression would have
intensified through the nineteenth century as plots were sold off for
building developments but large amounts of money continued to be spent
on ornamenting the house and gardens by Henry's great-grandson, the 4th
and last Lord Holland and his wife.

The Holland House estate was created in 1591 when Sir Walter Cope
(1553?–1614) purchased four manors to the west of London.[3] He built his
grand new house (called Cope's Castle, later Holland House) on Abbot's
Kensington land in 1604–1606 and laid out a pleasure ground around it.
The estate then covered about 500 acres and extended from what is now
Holland Park Avenue south almost to the river Thames.

The architectural and social history of Holland House itself is well-documented[4] but very little has been written about the park and pleasure grounds which surrounded it. There are gaps in the archive records but enough survives to show that, although at times neglected, they were laid out by owners with taste as well as money who were familiar, in their different times, with the finest gardens in England. Consequently, changing landscape fashions down the centuries were reflected in the gardens of Holland House. This book sets out to use the surviving evidence to create impressions of the gardens as they would have been seen and experienced in each of the four centuries of their existence. It starts with the Jacobean gardens and ends when the remaining grounds of the house (mortally injured in WWII bombing) were sold to the London County Council (LCC) for a public park. For those who visit and enjoy the Holland Park of today, we hope that this book will add a new dimension to your experience of it. Some elements of the old gardens remain or have been recreated in the park and although much more has disappeared under housing, there are still places to stand and imagine how the pleasure gardens of Holland House once looked.

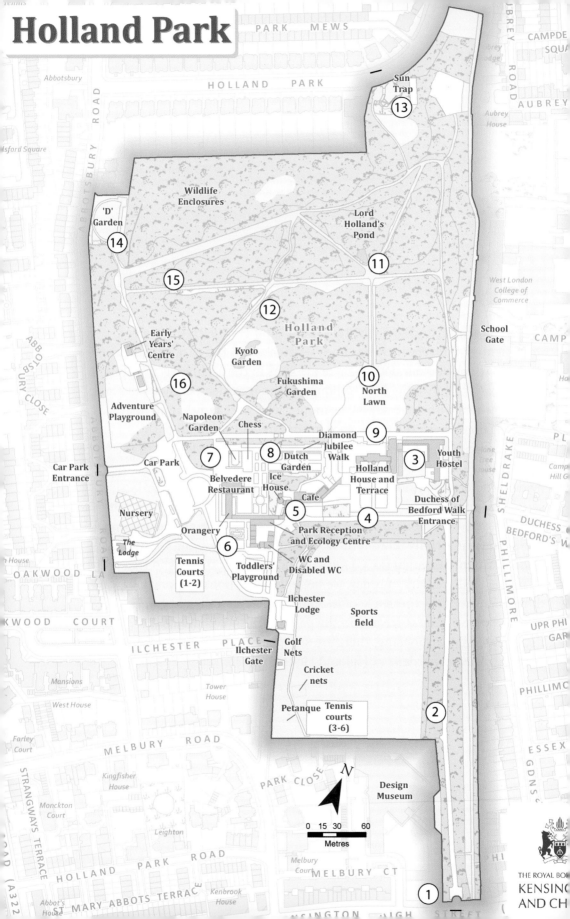

Holland Park

'PLACES TO STAND & IMAGINE'
A STROLL THROUGH THE HISTORIC LANDSCAPE OF HOLLAND PARK

1. THE ENTRANCE FROM KENSINGTON HIGH STREET

THE ATTRACTIVE ORNAMENTAL GATES, brought from Belgium, were erected in 1836 by the 3rd Lord Holland. They seem to be a pair of French eighteenth-century gates, much reworked, restored and extended. To the right is Holland Walk, originally part of the estate but given by Lord Holland as a public right of way in 1848 (in return for closing a public footpath across the front of the house). In the mid-eighteenth century this was the main entrance to the house. Where you are standing by the gates you would then have seen the toll bar and booth of the Kensington Turnpike Trust: those leaving London on this main route westwards had to pay a toll to use the road. The then owner, Henry Fox, travelling frequently between Westminster and his home, had the entrance made just in front of the toll gate to avoid paying. The other entrance to the estate was from the north end of Holland Walk, from the Acton Road (now Holland Park Avenue) which was the other main route west out of London.

See a view of the old entrance to Holland House on page 41.

Opposite: Map guide to the historic landscape of Holland Park

1

2.   ON THE PATH UP TO THE HOUSE

Stop and look to your left. All the land from Kensington High Street up to the house was part of the estate. In the seventeenth century it was called Munden Close and was divided into four fields, probably used as pasture and cut for hay. As the meadow it remained in use as hayfields with a perimeter belt of trees until the twentieth century (in the early twentieth century it occasionally hosted RHS Flower Shows). In 1922 it was laid out as an all-weather golf practice ground, later known rather more grandly as the Kensington Country Club. This was an attempt to raise income from the estate which had been heavily mortgaged in the nineteenth century.

See a map of the golf club on page 90.

During the Second World War the ground was used for Home Guard training and as a barrage balloon site, but by the time the London County Council acquired the estate for a public park in 1952, the trenched and bomb-cratered land was completely overgrown. Clearing it for use as a playing field was a priority and work started immediately. In 1960 the southern portion of the playing field became the site for the Commonwealth Institute, opened in 1962. This Grade II starred listed building has been empty and decaying since it closed in 2002. At the time of writing it is intended to be the new home of the Design Museum.

3.   THE KING GEORGE VI MEMORIAL YOUTH HOSTEL

The youth hostel was built in the 1950s, with new buildings grafted onto the surviving and restored Jacobean east front of the house to create a new courtyard and garden. By then this courtyard area was a rather derelict shrubbery with self-seeded sycamores but in the mid-eighteenth century there was an elegant bowling green here. In the mid-nineteenth century it became the grand entrance to the house. In 1848 the 4th Lord Holland re-oriented the house, moving the entrance from the south to the east front. Soil excavated to create the courtyard was used to build the terrace wall now seen across the south front. On the north wall of the courtyard an Italianate split stair above a fountain gave access to the higher level of the park behind. At the top of the stairs stood the seventeenth-century gate piers now seen at the entrance to the open air theatre (which occupies the footprint of the demolished house).

See a map of the courtyard on page 67.

The gate piers and steps giving access from the east courtyard to the gardens. Engraving from Princess Marie Liechenstein, Holland House *(London: 1874), vol. 1, p. 171.*

4. VIEW FROM THE GATE PIERS

Stand with your back to the gate piers at the theatre entrance and look down the playing field. You are standing on the central axis of the fine mansion built for Sir Walter Cope in 1604–6 and you would be looking down a grand central approach avenue lined with trees. The avenue stretched down to the 'Great Road' (Kensington High Street) and then on, still aligned on the centre of the house, through estate farm land to where the estate lands ended close to what is now Fulham Road.

See an earlier plan of the estate on page 16.

Now turn and look up at the gate piers, commissioned by Sir Henry Rich in 1629, made by Nicholas Stone and possibly designed by Inigo Jones. These piers have moved at least three times in their history: by 1752 if not earlier they stood at opposite corners of a railed entrance court. The terrace they now stand on was built in the 1840s to close off the old entrance courtyard.

See an early view of Holland House on page 39.

5. THE ARCADE AND STABLE YARD

As you walk on from the gate piers, on your right the terraced arcade once linked the house to the conservatory ahead. This Italianate arcade with terrace walk above was built in the 1840s by the 4th Lord Holland. As well as linking the house to the conservatory and the summer ballroom, used as entertainment areas, it also served to enclose the formal gardens behind. The conservatory and the summer ballroom occupy the site of Sir Henry Rich's stable block [see 7]. That was partially demolished in 1812 by the 3rd Lord Holland and a new stable block built. This is the stable yard you see today: as you enter the courtyard the stables were on the right, ahead were two double and one single coach houses, the other buildings were workshops and store rooms. The stables are currently occupied by the Ecology Centre: inside, the iron pillars which divided the stalls are now disguised as trees! (Fig. 26)

Read more about the changes made by the 3rd Lord Holland on pages 55–72.

The Summer Ballroom and the ivy-clad arches c. 1903.

6. 'SQUARE OF ORANGES' AND 'AQUEDUCT'

Turn the corner of the stables and walk past the toddlers' play area. The square of ground south of the conservatory (now known as the orangery) is a rose garden. A hundred years ago this was where orange trees in their tubs would be moved from the conservatory in the summer months.

See a view of the 'square of oranges' on page 38.

Walk on round past the Belvedere Restaurant (which now occupies the conservatory) and to the line of brick arches. These were formerly part of the stable block demolished in 1812. The arches were left as they were thought to suggest the ruins of an aqueduct, and they were clad with ivy for a picturesque effect. In front of them the hard surfaced area with benches was where the 3rd Lady Holland raised some of the first dahlias to be grown in England, in the early 1800s. Later, the area was laid out as an Italian terrace garden. (Fig. 52)

7.   Sir Henry Rich's magnificent stable block

The arches and the wall of the Belvedere Restaurant represent the back wall of the magnificent stables and coach houses, possibly designed by Inigo Jones and built by Sir Henry Rich around 1638. This was a display of status and wealth at a cost of £4000, the equivalent of a complete country house for a less ambitious courtier.

Read more about Sir Henry Rich on pages 25–27.

8.   The formal gardens

The formal gardens here were first laid out in 1812 as an Italian garden of parterres and fountains on the site of the old stable yard. They were designed to be seen from the west wing of the house. The 3rd Lord Holland and his wife had travelled and lived in Italy, spoke Italian and Holland House was host to many distinguished Italian visitors. They were also admirers of Napoleon and in the hedged compartment nearest the arches (where today there is a changing art installation) they placed a bust of Napoleon on a marble pillar (since lost). Napoleon faced a fountain and behind the fountain the alcove (a fireplace in Henry Rich's stable block) now know as Roger's Seat.

See a sketch of Napoleon on his pillar on page 61.

Later in the century the formal gardens became more ornate with acute-angled beds planted in summer with massed bedding in bright colours and variously described as the Italian, Dutch or even Portuguese garden, such was the confusion about garden styles at the end of the nineteenth century.

9.   The terrace behind the house

In the seventeenth century from this spot you would look across a terrace to a plainly turfed formal parterre with a central pool, flanked by small

The Dutch Garden seen from the Summer Ballroom during a garden party, c. 1894.

orchards and avenues. To the left a large walled kitchen garden and ahead a crossing avenue of trees, the whole enclosed by high brick walls, as described in Sir Walter Cope's will. The present view of lawns and trees rising gently from the back of the house dates from the mid-eighteenth century, when the owner Henry Fox swept away the earlier formal gardens. Henry Fox also changed the access routes to the house and the wide path here which bisects the park follows the line of his northern access to the stables. In the early nineteenth century, as part of the design for the new formal gardens and the removal of the old stables, this drive was relaid as a path with its double flight of Italianate steps.

See a plan of the Jacobean garden and read more about it on pages 30–32.

10. THE NORTH LAWN

From 1746 Henry Fox began planting native and exotic (mainly North American) trees in clumps and as specimens in open glades and lawns behind the house. His friend from schooldays, Charles Hamilton of Painshill, advised on the planting and Quaker cloth merchant and naturalist Peter Collinson supplied many tree seeds from his trading contacts in North America. As late as 1937 three of Henry Fox's cedars still stood on the north lawn, but it is unlikely that any other trees planted by him still survive. There is one old cedar in the park, in the north-east corner just inside a gate marked 'staff only'. It is probably about 140 years old, which suggests it was part of the extensive re-planting done by the 5th Earl of Ilchester after he acquired the estate in 1874.

See a plan of Henry Fox's park on page 44 and read more about his collaboration with Hamilton and Collinson on pages 46–54.

11. THE WILDERNESS

The azalea walk beyond the north lawn was a rose garden in the nineteenth century planted with a Victorian favourite, the pink Mme Caroline Testout. At the top is a pond and the statue of the 3rd Lord Holland, admirer of all things Italian. The avenues which radiate from this spot on the crest of the hill lie on the footprint of a much earlier feature, a Wilderness of eight *allées* in a star shape with a central open grove decorated with statuary. It was probably laid out in the late seventeenth century, before formality in gardens began to give way to the English landscape style. 'Wilderness' then meant a designed and ornamental grove of trees in straight lines, cut to frame views of the garden or the surrounding countryside. It was somewhere to stroll and talk, closer to 'nature' than the very formal spaces nearer the house. The Wilderness disappeared over a period of two hundred years but the present avenues were re-planted in the early nineteenth century by the 5th Earl of Ilchester. A view is still framed (especially in winter) by the path which runs downhill to the north-east corner of the park.

See how the Wilderness changed over its lifetime on pages 37 and 38.

The top tank of the water garden.

12. The Water garden

From Lord Holland's statue turn to your left to the gate into the Oak Enclosure. This area, where pigs sometimes help to clear the ground in summer, is not open to the public. But at the turn of the nineteenth century there was a water garden here where spring water ran between square brick tanks built to grow and display the recently introduced hardy water lilies, and other aquatic plants. If the ground is clear you should see the first tank at least.

For more about the water garden and the planting see pages 73–78.

13. The 'suntrap' entrance

When the estate was still in private hands there were no additional entrances in the northern boundary. When it became a public park, new entrances were needed for public access. The entrance at No. 1 Holland Park, with the sun terraces and the grass plat above, was built between 1954 and 1956, when the boundary wall was rebuilt. It was officially opened in 1958. Originally there was a squash court on the grass plat; after the building had to be demolished because of subsidence, the area was then used for a while as a petanque court.

14. The 'D' Garden

The second new entrance, which is called the 'D' garden for its shape, was built and laid out in 1953 as a formal garden of trees, shrubs and herbaceous plants. That planting has been retained. The tortoises and sundial are a more recent addition.

15. The Lime Tree Avenue

This was first planted in 1876 by the Dowager Lady Holland, although the 5th Earl of Ilchester paid for it. Most of the limes blew down in the storm of 1987 and have since been completely replaced by The Friends of Holland Park. Many of the mature trees you see today in the park were planted by the Earl of Ilchester, who funded a lot of restoration and replanting. Happily, he also saved the remaining 55 acres of the original estate from development (a real threat in the early 1900s) and so enabled you to enjoy the park today.

Take a walk through the gardens in 1937 on pages 73–91.

16. The Japanese Garden

In the early 1900s the water garden was extended to create an 'Anglo-Japanese' garden, below and a little to the west of, the present Kyoto Japanese garden, finishing opposite to what is now the entrance to the adventure playground. At that time Japanese gardens were very fashionable, but the idea was rather vague: if a garden had water, a few rocks and some exotic planting, it was called Japanese, although much of the planting would be very English. The most famous one was at Gunnersbury Park.

See more photographs of the first Japanese garden on pages 80–82.

These gardens were a collaboration between the 5th Earl of Ilchester and his head gardener Charles Dixon, a fellow of the RHS. The Japanese garden had rimmed oval-shaped pools with large stepping stones crossing them. Quite a lot of the rockwork can still be seen. From the gate opposite the Adventure Playground looking up the slope you will see some of it when the vegetation is low in the winter and spring.

From 1823 plots of land from the estate were sold off for building, but beneath the streets that adjoin the park today there is a lot more garden history! It is all recorded in this book.

View of the line of ponds in the Japanese garden.

Some of the surviving rockwork from the ponds.

CHRONOLOGY OF OWNERSHIP

1599–1614	Sir Walter Cope.
1614–1621	Dorothy, widow of Sir Walter.
1621–1649	Sir Henry Rich, 1st Earl of Holland, Cope's son-in-law After the Civil War the estate was restored to Rich's widow and their son Robert.
1655–1675	Robert, 2nd Earl of Holland.
1675–1701	Edward, 3rd Earl of Holland .
1701–1721	Edward Henry, 4th Earl of Holland. Died without heir.
1721–1746	Estate passed to the Edwardes family (descendants of Henry Rich). House let to tenants.
1746–1774	Henry Fox. Created 1st Baron Holland (of Foxley, Wiltshire) in 1763.
1774–1840	Henry Richard Fox, 3rd Lord Holland (Henry Fox's grandson).
1840–1845	Elizabeth, Lady Holland, widow.
1845–1859	Henry Edward, 4th Lord Holland.
1859–1874	Augusta, Lady Holland, widow. Although estate sold in 1874 she remained in residence until her death in 1889.
1874–1905	Henry Edward Fox-Strangways, 5th Earl of Ilchester, direct descendant of Stephen, older brother of Henry Fox.
1905–1952	Giles Stephen Holland Fox-Strangways, 6th Earl of Ilchester.
1952	House and remaining land sold to London County Council.

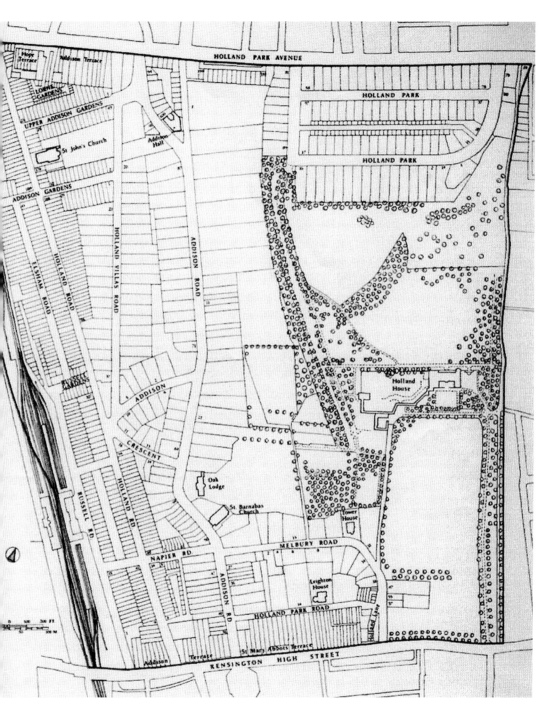

1. The Holland estate: the thick line shows the boundaries of the estate purchased by Henry Fox in 1768, superimposed on the OS survey of 1894–6.

1599–1675
'Places of Pleasure'

W ALTER COPE WAS THE THIRD SON of a gentleman
farmer near Banbury, Oxfordshire. He entered Grays Inn in 1570
and shortly became gentleman usher to William Cecil, later Lord
Burghley. Under Burghley's patronage he became an official of the Court
of Wards in 1574 and obtained other official, lucrative posts in the
following years.[5] He continued to serve Burghley, being described as his
secretary in 1593. He also became a friend and acolyte of Burghley's son
Robert Cecil, a relationship which continued after Burghley's death in
1598. He was knighted in 1603 on the accession of James I, having been in
the party that travelled north to welcome the king and he advanced in
favour in James's court, rising to become Chamberlain of the Exchequer
in 1609.[6] Sir Walter's increasing wealth enabled him to acquire land west
of London, creating by 1599 an estate of some 500 acres which extended
from what is now Holland Park Avenue south almost to the Fulham Road
and the river Thames. As an influential courtier and wealthy man he
needed a suitably grand house and in 1604–06 he built a mansion,
probably to designs by John Thorpe.[7] It was known as Cope's Castle (later
Kensington House then Holland House). There was a building boom from
the 1580s in peaceful times which lasted into the 1620s. The need for
country estates to be defensible and self-sufficient sites (with walls, moats
and service buildings close to the house) gave way to new ideas about the
relationship between the house and its setting in the landscape.

THE HOUSE IN ITS SETTING

It is likely that, reflecting the new ideas, Cope's Castle was approached by a long straight entrance avenue aligned on the central axis of the house, leading into at least one forecourt. It was a rather more modest building than the 'princely palace' for which Francis Bacon prescribed a prolonged approach, leading to three entrance courts: an outer plain green (turfed) court, a second more ornamental green court and an inner court, squared with the front and enclosed by terraces.[8] There is an estate survey of 1694/5, done for Edward, 3rd Earl of Holland (1675–1701), Sir Walter's great-grandson. The original is lost but it was copied in 1734.[9] The purpose of the copy, as recorded on the plan, was to update fences and boundaries and record the tenants then occupying the estate (Figs 1 and 2).[10] It is not possible to say for certain that no other changes were made to the original

2. Detail from the 1694/5 survey: the cartouche
recording the purpose of the copy.

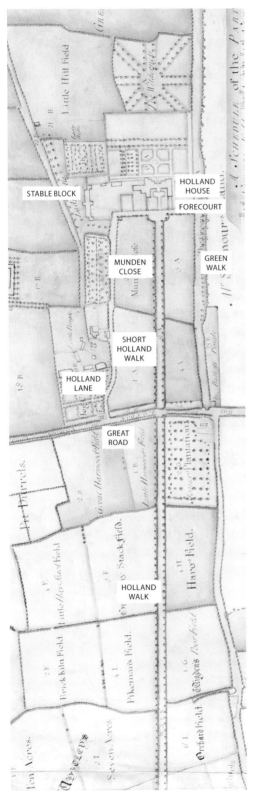

STABLE BLOCK

HOLLAND HOUSE

FORECOURT

MUNDEN CLOSE

GREEN WALK

SHORT HOLLAND WALK

HOLLAND LANE

GREAT ROAD

HOLLAND WALK

survey but the copy does show a right angled extension to the west wing of the mansion added around 1640 that was demolished in 1704.[11] This suggests that the survey had not been updated and the 1734 copy probably shows the house in its original setting. This survey will be referred to again, as the '1694/5 survey'.

A tree-lined avenue aligned on the central axis of the house runs from the 'Great Road' (later the Kensington Turnpike, now Kensington High Street) through 'Munden Close' (the piece of land now occupied by the playing field and the former Commonwealth Institute site) (Fig. 3). Munden Close is quartered into meadows and would have offered a long, rising approach view of the house. This section of the avenue is called 'Short Holland Walk'. At the north end a semi-circle edged with trees gives on to a cross path running in front of the house. Along the east side of Munden Close 'The Green Walk' runs from the Great Road to the 'Road from London to Uxbridge' (now Holland Park Avenue). This was almost certainly a public right of way. Along the west side of Munden Close another lane, named as 'Holland Lane', leads off the Great Road and gives

3. Detail from the 1694/5 survey, showing the approaches to the house. Author's annotation.

another route to the house and stables. It seems likely that this was the functional everyday access route to the house, while Short Holland Walk would have been reserved for family and guests. Depending on the land available, approach avenues to the great Tudor houses were often projected out into the countryside. At Holland House, the tree-lined avenue continues south of the Great Road and as 'Holland Walk' runs straight, through estate land, still aligned with the centre of the house, ending close to where 'The Sewer' empties into Chelsea creek through a sluice. [12]

SIR WALTER'S WATER GARDEN

Having built a grand house and approach it is inconceivable that Sir Walter did not lay out pleasure grounds around it. In this more secure and relaxed time gardening became a recreation, in some cases a passion for many of the aristocracy and landed gentry and an extensive pleasure garden was an essential adjunct of any great house: walks and arbors, terraces, mounts, bowling greens, orchards and water gardens. Medieval fish ponds were adapted into Elizabethan water gardens which gave way to an Italian-inspired fashion for fountains, grottos and *giochi d'acqua* (literally 'water-jokes' designed to soak the unwary) which often incorporated automata. Such gardens were often made on the site of medieval stew ponds as that was where the most convenient water supply was likely to be, and these were often some distance from the house: Francis Bacon's water garden at his house at Gorhambury in Hertfordshire, made around 1608, was one mile from the house at the end of a tree-lined Long Walk.[13] They would still be practical (holding fish for the table) but the aesthetic value of water in a garden was increasingly appreciated.

Sir Walter would have been familiar with some of the great gardens of the late sixteenth and early seventeenth centuries created by the aristocracy and courtiers and here his connection with William Cecil becomes significant. Theobolds in Hertfordshire was the most important Elizabethan garden 'perfected most costly, bewtyfully, & pleasantly' and it was made by Burghley between 1575 and 1585. His 'greatest greatness

4. *William Cecil, Lord Burghley in his garden at Theobalds.*

and only happiness' (according to his biographer) was 'riding in his garden walks, upon his little mule'.[14] In a delightful, intimate portrait of him doing just that (the only one not to show him in sombre black gowns) he is holding a nosegay of gillyflowers and honeysuckle and the landscape around him is filled with wild flowers in bloom (Fig. 4).

He encompassed the pleasure gardens at Theobolds with a maze of canals. A visitor described it in 1598, the canal 'large enough for one to have the pleasure of going in a boat, and even rowing between the shrubs'.[15] Burghley's son Robert added an artificial river 'that was better than if natural', ponds and islands in 1602–3.[16] It seems that Sir Walter Cope paid a visit there in 1602 as a personal errand for Robert Cecil to help resolve problems with the spring water feed.[17] So Sir Walter knew Theobolds; he would have been familiar with the varying styles of water gardens then in fashion, from formal and geometric to more 'natural'. A water garden might have been an essential adjunct to his new mansion, especially as he entertained King James and Queen Anne there.[18]

In 1820 there is a reference to the 'Moats or fish ponds' still in evidence at the end of the eighteenth century, the site:

> formerly intersected with gravel walks; and the islands, which are in the middle of the ponds, were connected with wooden bridges. Of late years the ponds have been cleaned and the sluices repaired, and at present they are well-stocked with fish: these ponds are supplied from an adjoining perennial spring of excellent water.[19]

This description, of gravel walks and islands in the ponds is characteristic of early seventeenth-century water gardens. The site is given as about a quarter of a mile from the house, towards Hammersmith, and in the adjoining kitchen garden was still standing part of the 'ancient Manor House of "West Town", converted into a residence for the gardener'.[20] The restoration would have been done by Henry Richard, 3rd Baron Holland. The 1694/5 survey shows the location of the ponds, aligned north–south, in relation to the house and its gardens, in the position described (Fig. 5).

To the east of the line of ponds a moat encloses a square of land planted as an orchard with one access point. Around the outside of the moat is a double line of trees and a tree-lined walk leads towards the site. The enlarged view (Fig. 6) shows the line of ponds enclosed and divided by paths with semi-circular, square and round projections into the ponds. The site is bordered by a narrow canal on the west and south sides.

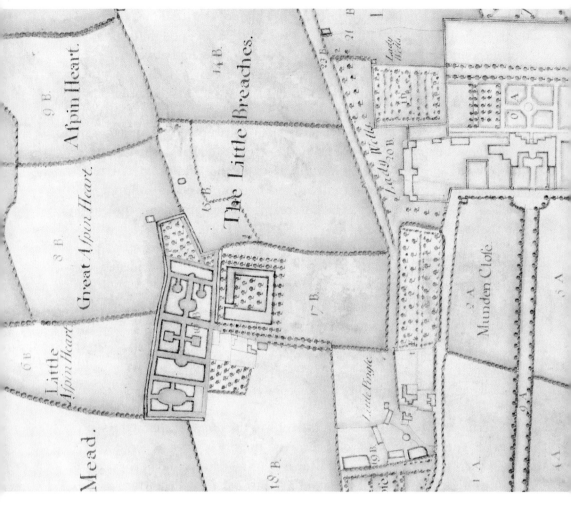

9 B.

Afpin Heart.

8 B.

Great Afpin Heart.

6 B

Little
Afpin Heart

Mead.

14 B.

The Little Breaches.

15 B.

0

17 B.

18 B.

Little Pingle

10 B

23 B. 22 21 B

Lady
Well

3B.19 20 B

3 A

Munden Clofe.

3 A

1 A.

5. *Detail from the 1694/5 survey, showing the position of the ponds or 'Water Maze' in relation to the house.*

To the north the canal extends to enclose an orchard alongside a path. In the north-west corner there is a square which may be the cistern for the spring feed. The legend to the plan lists this area (16B) as 'The Ponds or Water Maze' (Fig. 7) and the area given is just over four acres. Another long narrow canal separates the ponds from the moated orchard.

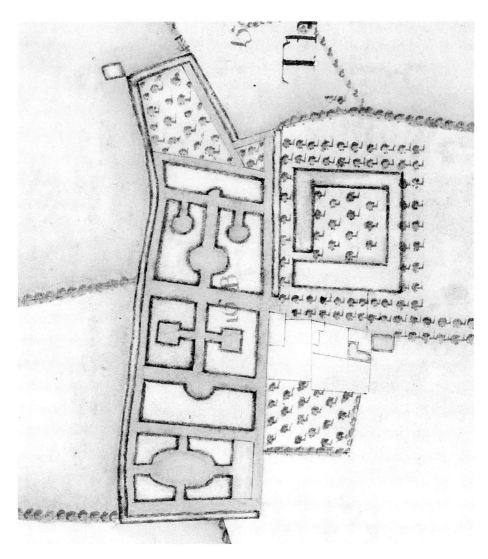

*6. Detail from the 1694/5 survey, showing the 'Water Maze'.
North to the top.*

*7. Detail from the Legend to the 1694/5 survey: The Ponds or Water Maze (16) and
Moat & Field adjoining (17).*

14	The Little Breaches			3	11		John V
15	Ditto. nom 2 Fields		8	2	22	1	The. b
16	The Ponds or Water Maze		4	1	8	2	Pt of
17	Moat & Field adjoing		5	2	10	3	Pt of
18	Ponds House & Field adjoining		10	1	18		
19	Hog Close and Little Breach		8	2	0		Thom

This layout looks too grand and complex to be associated with the remaining part of the manor house shown below the square moat, but if this is where the water source was it is likely that there were earlier fish ponds or stews here. A smaller scale survey plan of 1717 (of which only a poor quality copy remains)[21] shows a moated garden lying about a quarter of a mile south west of the house divided by paths into quarters, a tree lined avenue leading towards it. Two other eighteenth-century maps also show rectangular ponds in the right location, but in much less detail.[22]

It cannot be said for certain that this whole complex was an Elizabethan or Jacobean water garden created by Walter Cope: although one writer quotes 'old books' as recording that 'the garden round the old Manor House was laid out in Elizabeth's reign', no corroborating documentary evidence has yet been found.[23] But the similarity with existing plans for such gardens is suggestive, for example in Gervase Markham's *Cheape and Good Husbandry* (1623) there are designs for water gardens with round, square and triangular projections into the ponds.

The water gardens created in the early seventeenth century were places for the owner and his guests to retreat from a busy household, to relax and enjoy the natural world with a degree of comfort. Francis Bacon wrote a description of the water garden he intended to build at Gorhambury. Espaliered fruit trees were to be grown on the inside of the walls and a terrace would overlook 'a fine little stream rune upon gravel and fine peppell [pebble]' with a walk on the other side that formed the boundary of a lake inside. There were to be eight islands, one with a summer house 'for freshnes' with dining room and bed chamber and a 'Roome for Musike'. The smaller islands were accessible only by boat and each was to have a special feature: a 'standing' in a tree [tree-house]; a 'Grott' [grotto], a Mount with 'flowers in ascents'; an arbour of musk roses, and more.[24] A visitor to a water garden at Hatfield House wrote of seats placed so that 'you may see a vast Number of Fish pass to and fro in the Water, which is exceedingly clear; and they seem to come in shoals to enjoy all the Pleasures of the Place; and quitting their own Element by jumping sometimes out of the Water, this they do as it were to observe all the things I have describ'd to you'.[25] We can imagine strolling with Sir

Walter the quarter mile from his house, down the slope and into a tree-lined avenue through the fields to reach his cool, refreshing, 'place of pleasure'.

WALLED GARDENS AND ORCHARDS

Before the Civil War, travel in France, Italy and Holland fostered an interest in and exchange of knowledge about the new plants arriving in Europe. Through his connection with the Cecils Sir Walter knew John Tradescant (the Elder). In the autumn/winter of 1611 Tradescant went on a plant-buying spree through the Low Countries and France for Robert Cecil. His total purchases for Cecil in Leiden, Haarlem and Delft amounted to £34. But he was also carrying £38 from Cope, for purchasing trees. For Cecil he bought tulips, snakes-head fritillaries and jonquils and fruit trees including early ripening cherries, Spanish pear, 'apple quince', mulberries. Trees and shrubs included limes, 'Arborvitae' (*Thuja occidentalis*) and *Daphne mezereum*.[26] We can assume that the trees brought back for Kensington were a similar mix. Orchards captured the aristocratic imagination, providing a setting for courtly indulgence, a favoured place for walking and sensuous enjoyment. Robert Dudley at Kenilworth had Elizabeth's confectioners' candy apple blossom on the trees so that she could have the pleasure of plucking them to eat as she strolled in the orchard there. In 1623 William Lawson wrote a paean to the orchard which suggests planting with roses, woodbine, cowslips, primrose, violet, rosemary and eglantine under 'walks set with great wood' for the 'honest delight of the owner and his friends'.[27] Sir Walter certainly had orchards: in July 1608 a visitor recorded: 'On Tuesday I went with the Lady Fanshawe and other good company to visit Cope's Castle at Kensington. We had the honour to see all, but touch nothing, not so much as a cherry, which are charily preserved for the Queen's coming'.[28] The choice of words suggests that the gardens at Cope's Castle were impressive. The practice of forcing or keeping back fruit to impress an important visitor made skilled gardeners highly sought after. In late summer 1600 Elizabeth paid a visit to Beddington Park in Surrey, home of Sir Francis Carew, whose gardener had held back the cherries from ripening (by covering the trees with canvas) so that she could enjoy them

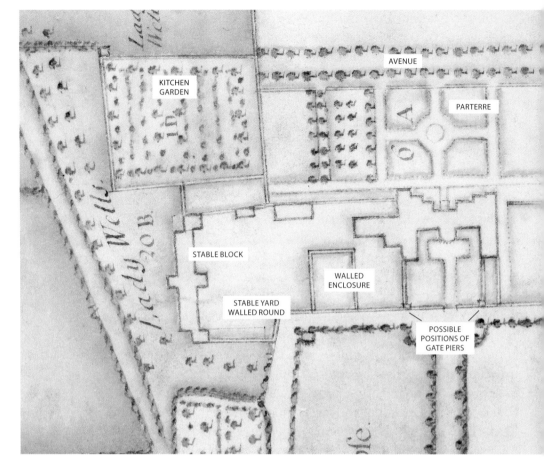

8. Detail from the 1694/5 survey : layout of the courtyards around the house. Author's annotation.

at their best.[29] Beddington Park, incidentally, also had a magnificent French-inspired water garden.

We have little information about the rest of Sir Walter's pleasure garden and park, although there are a few hints in his will.[30] It refers to 'all edifices, houses, barnes, stables, gardens, orchards, yards and courtyards, within the utmost Bricke wall of the sayd House', which tells us that these areas, about 12 acres in all, were enclosed by a brick wall and that there was more than one orchard close to the house, as well as the moated orchard a quarter of a mile away in the fields. These features can still be seen in the 1694/5 survey: the brick walls (in red) enclose the house, yards and kitchen garden (Fig 8).

The house has a walled forecourt, its entrance aligned with Short Holland Walk. The entrance to the forecourt would be the site for the stone gate piers built by Nicholas Stone in 1629 for Henry Rich: '2 peeres [piers]of good Portland stone to hang a pair of great wooden gates on for £100'.[31] No gate or gate piers are shown here but small square structures are shown at the bottom right and left corners of the forecourt, so the gate piers may by then have been moved to the position in which they are seen in later views.[32] This forecourt is a 'green court' with a hedged approach path through it widening into a rectangle in front of the house entrance. A further rectangular enclosed courtyard to the east is aligned on the east wing of the house and beyond that is another partially walled courtyard. To the west of the house stands the huge stable block and courtyard completely enclosed by walls. Between house and stable block there is a separate oblong walled yard. There are two other buildings along the north wall. The walls are continuous – no entrances to the stable courtyard are shown, although they must have existed!

Henry Rich's stables

Although at the end of his life Sir Walter died in debt as a result of market speculation, in 1612 he was rich and well-connected enough to marry his only child and heiress Isabel (also called Elizabeth) to Sir Henry Rich (1590–1649), later Earl of Holland. In his will Sir Walter left his house and estate to 'Dame Dorothie, my well beloved wife', but when she remarried in 1621 the estate passed to Isabel and her husband. However Rich would have been responsible for the property on behalf of his mother-in-law (who died in 1638) and wife. Henry Rich (Fig. 9) was a handsome, flamboyant and fashionable courtier to both James I and Charles I. He had a penchant for political dealings (and other relationships) with many women: Marie d'Medici; Anne of Austria (Queen of Louis XIII), Queen Henrietta Maria and many of her court ladies, notably the Countess of Carlisle, but his public life was largely one of frustrated ambition.[33]

His improvements to Holland House were done when he 'retired to his house at Kensington in disgust' at failing to obtain the post of Lord High Admiral.[34] Between 1638 and 1640 he added a brick wing at right angles to the centre of the west wing of the house, seen in Fig. 8.[35] At the same

9. The gorgeously suited Sir Henry Rich, First Earl of Holland, c. 1632–33, school of Daniel Mytens.

time he spent the huge sum of £4000 (the equivalent of a complete country house for a less ambitious courtier) on the magnificent stables and coach house west of the house. Such structures, in the seventeenth century, were far more than utilitarian buildings: like terraces, banqueting houses and water gardens they were symbols of display and ambition. This building, which stood until 1812, would have been among the finest anywhere in England and it may have been designed by Inigo Jones (Figs 10 & 11). Henry Rich certainly knew him, having ten years earlier commissioned the gate piers made by Nicholas Stone, the design of which is attributed to Jones.[36]

But building works apart, between court intrigue, diplomatic and other royal missions to Europe and an intermittent military career, it seems

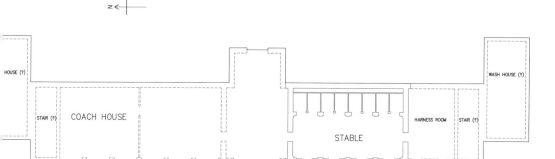

HOUSE (?)

STAIR (?) COACH HOUSE

STABLE

HARNESS ROOM STAIR (?)

WASH HOUSE (?)

-10 0 10 20 30 40 50
FEET
-5 0 5 10 15
METRES

10. Henry Rich's stables. Reconstructed plan of the stable and coach house range, based on a partial survey of 1796.

11. Reconstructed west elevation of the stable block, with coach house to the north (left) and stables to the south (right).

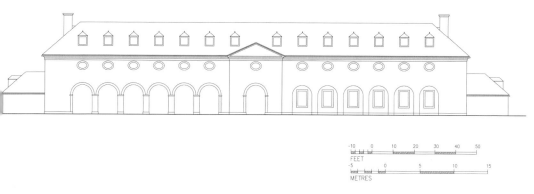

-10 0 10 20 30 40 50
FEET
-5 0 5 10 15
METRES

unlikely that Henry Rich had much time for the gardens at Holland House and there is no evidence of any major changes. His political allegiances were always suspect, he flipped from side to side in the Civil War and, inevitably, lost his head in 1649. The house had been briefly occupied as his headquarters by General Sir Thomas Fairfax during the Civil War but it was later returned to Rich's widow. She died there in 1655. Her son Robert (?1620–1675) inherited. It is likely that, in common with many other estates at that time, the house and gardens were by then in a run-down condition.

1675–1746
WILDERNESS AND
FORMALITY

THE PERIOD AFTER THE RESTORATION saw the creation of many great gardens by royalty and the aristocracy, partly French influenced. The style was formal with straight canals, long avenues which often extended far into the parkland, groves, or *bosquets* and wildernesses. At Holland House Edward, 3rd Earl of Holland (?1673–1701) succeeded his father Robert in 1675. In 1701 Edward died, leaving a widow, Lady Warwick, and the three year old Edward Henry, 4th Earl. In 1716 Lady Warwick married Joseph Addison, one of the famous names associated with Holland House. Addison was an influential writer on gardens, however he died at Holland House in 1719 after a long period of ill health and seems not to have had any impact on the gardens.

Any major changes to the garden during this period are likely to have occurred during the last decades of seventeenth century, and the survey of 1694/5 shows us the gardens at that time. The most striking feature is the star-shaped Wilderness on the rising ground to the north of the house for which Edward, the 3rd Earl may have been responsible. The Wilderness degraded and disappeared over the following three hundred years but its ghost remains in the line of five of the original eight paths: they meet where the statue of the 3rd Lord Holland now stands.

THE WILDERNESS

'Wilderness' was a term for a designed grove or wood with paths cut through it, an ornamental area designed for walking and admiring the views out into the countryside and it was usually laid out at a distance from the house. The design would be geometric and the star was quite a common one. In the early eighteenth century this formality began to give way to winding paths and later still, a wilderness would be an informal woodland of mixed species.[37]

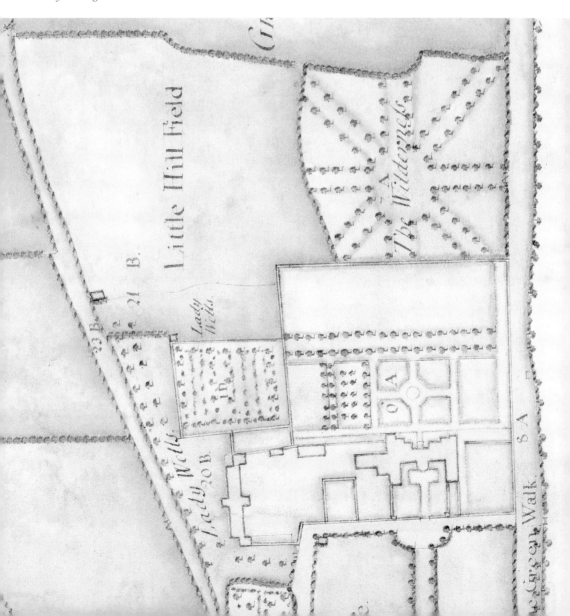

12. Detail from the 1694/5 survey showing the Wilderness to the north of the house and its formal gardens.

Contemporary descriptions of Wildernesses appear from 1600. At Francis Bacon's estate at Gorhambury the Wilderness was described as a rectangular enclosure of fifteen acres, 'coppice-wood where there are walks cutt-out as straight as a line, and broade enough for a coach, a quarter mile long or better'.[38] While more modest in scale, the position and layout of the Wilderness at Holland House suggest that it could date from early in the century (so a survival from Sir Walter Cope's time). But it seems more likely that it was laid out after the Restoration so it will be discussed here. Our first view of it is in the survey of 1694/5 where it looks pristine (Fig. 12).

The survey gives the area of the Wilderness as just over 5 acres. Eight allées lead towards a circular open grove and the north-south axis is aligned on the house. The allées are composed of single lines of trees but as the area of the Wilderness is irregular, the length of each allée varies, being shortest on the south side (towards the house) and longest on the north-east side. The trees are regularly spaced and number from three to eight pairs in each allée: they were mostly 'lofty elms & sycamores'.[39] The Wilderness is hedged on the east, north and west sides but on the south side is bounded by a brick wall which divides it from the formal gardens of the house. There does not appear to be a gate in the wall, instead the entrance seems to be on the east side, off the Green Walk. The position of the open grove was determined by being the highest point on the rise from the house affording the best views out over the surrounding countryside, the land falling away to the north and west. It is difficult for us now to envisage the extent of those views, but in 1698 the well-travelled Celia Fiennes was on the leads of Windsor Castle Tower from where she could see 'the country round to Kensington; I could see Lord of Holland's house and rows of trees'.[40]

The gardens within the 'utmost Bricke wall'

The survey of 1694/5 shows the layout of the rest of the garden (Fig. 12). On the north front a broad terrace overlooks a formal parterre with a central circular pond. This parterre appears to be of plain unornamented turf (the liking for which had persisted from earlier in the century) rather than the more elaborate 'embroidered' parterres such as the one made at Hampton Court in 1690 for William III. To the west a tree-lined path separates a small orchard from another plain rectangle of turf. The terrace is closed by a brick wall which forms one side of the kitchen garden (marked ID on the plan). Turning east the terrace continues to a wall separating the garden from the Green Walk: a path continues north along the wall. Although the wall was later replaced with an avenue of trees, the line of this path survives today. The north side of the formal garden is bounded by a wall, with four openings in it. A formal avenue lies east-west and beyond that the garden extends as a plain turfed area to the boundary wall. Beyond that wall is the Wilderness. The fact that there is no entrance into the Wilderness here suggests that the wall pre-dates it. Looking at the plan we can see that the whole area occupied by the house, its forecourts and stable yard, the kitchen garden, the formal gardens and avenues is enclosed by a brick wall. This almost certainly had survived since Sir Walter's time and is the wall referred to in his will: 'all edifices, houses, barnes, stables, gardens, orchards, yards and courtyards, within the circuit of the utmost Bricke wall of the sayd house'.[41] By the end of the seventeenth century the gardens within the old brick walls would have looked rather old-fashioned. The Wilderness was a new and fashionable addition, extending the pleasure grounds into the fields.

THE NEW CENTURY

Edward died in 1701 and his widow, in 1716, married Joseph Addison (1672–1719). Addison was, in the early years of the century, a very influential writer on gardens at a time when gardening was a political (there were 'Whig' and 'Tory' gardens) as well as fashionable activity for cultivated men. In a series of essays in *The Spectator* (which he co-founded in 1711) he described his idea of the perfect garden, where Reason and Nature go hand in hand, and works of nature are 'more delightful than artificial shows', thus rejecting the lingering formality of the previous century.[42] In 1713 he purchased Bilton Hall, an estate near Rugby with 1000 acres of land, allowing this city man to re-invent himself as lord of the manor and improver of the landscape.[43] In a *Spectator* essay he described his garden at Bilton: 'It is a Confusion of Kitchin and Parterre, Orchard and Flower Garden, which lie so mixt and interwoven with one another, that if a Foreigner, who had seen nothing of our Country, should be conveyed into my Garden at his first landing, he would look upon it as a natural Wilderness, and one of the uncultivated parts of our Country'.[44] However, it seems the gardens at Bilton were laid out with more formal symmetry than this description of it would suggest.[45]

When, in middle age, Addison married Charlotte, Lady Warwick, they had known each other since at least 1705 and her son, Edward Henry, became a protégé of Addison. Two surviving letters he wrote to the boy in 1708 suggest a companionable relationship.

> My dearest Lord,
>
> I can't forbear being troublesome to your Lordship whilst I am in your neighbourhood.[46] The business of this is to invite you to a concert of music, which I have found out in a neighbouring wood. It begins precisely at six in the evening, and consists of a black-bird, a thrush, a robin-red-breast, and a bull-finch. There is a lark, that, by way of over-ture, sings and mounts till she is almost out of hearing; ...the whole is conducted by a nightingale, that has a much better voice than Mrs Tofts, and something of Italian manners in her divisions...[47]

Addison's health declined rapidly from 1718 and he died at Holland House in June 1719 at the age of 47. There seems to be no evidence that during the brief three years of marriage and public service as Secretary of State he made any changes to the gardens at Holland House. His writings about nature in the garden presaged the English landscape style but he did not live to see those ideas put into practice.

Addison's *protégé*, Tickell,[48] wrote a rather Homeric poem on Addison's death, evoking the pleasures of the Holland House gardens and in particular the extensive and airy prospect over the surrounding countryside:

> Thou hill! whose brow the antique sculptures grace
> Rear'd by bold chiefs of Warwick's noble race;
> Why scene so lov'd! where e'er thy bow'r appears
> O'er my dim eye-balls glance the sudden tears?
> How sweet were once thy prospects fresh and fair
> Thy sloping walls, and unpolluted air!

How sweet the gloom beneath thy aged trees,
Thy noon-tide shadow, and thy ev'ning breeze,
His image thy forsaken bow'rs restore,
Thy walks and airy prospects charm no more;
No more, the Summer in thy glooms allay'd,
Thy ev'ning breezes and thy noon-day shade.

The first two lines suggest that the open grove at the centre of the Wilderness (at the brow of the hill) was ornamented with classical statuary some time after 1673 (when the title Earl of Warwick was inherited by the 2nd Earl Holland). In 1721 Edward Henry, 4th and last Earl, died childless at the age of 24 and the estate passed to William Edwardes, a great-grandson of Sir Henry Rich. There is no evidence that any member of the Edwardes family lived at Holland House. It was let to a variety of tenants (as recorded on the 1734 copy of the 1694/5 survey) and the gardens at best kept in order. Little would have changed until Henry Fox took the property in 1746.

1746–1774
HENRY FOX'S GARDEN

HENRY FOX (1705–1774), POLITICIAN, created 1st Baron Holland of Foxley in 1763, took a lease on the then probably rather run-down Holland estate in 1746, purchasing it in 1763. He made major changes to the approaches to the house, both for convenience and privacy. Fox was keen to improve the pleasure grounds and from 1750 drew on the advice of close friend and innovative garden-maker Charles Hamilton of Painshill and naturalist Peter Collinson, planting a landscape park with both native trees and the sought-after new introductions from North America. In the 1760s Hamilton advised on the layout of an ornamented 'Green Lane' which, running between the park and the fields of the estate had elements of the *ferme ornée* style which was fashionable in the mid-eighteenth century. When he took the estate older features had survived in the Holland House gardens. Henry Fox swept much away, creating a landscape with elements still recognisable today.

In 1744 Henry Fox eloped with and married Lady (Georgiana) Caroline Lennox, against the will of her parents, the Duke and Duchess of Richmond. In 1746 he leased Holland House as their country home, having recently been promoted to the office of Secretary at War. He had a lucrative income from political office, a fortune hugely enlarged by speculating with the vast balances of public money that passed through his hands as paymaster during the Seven Years' War (1756–1763): an activity then quite legal![49] He spent freely on improving Holland House and its grounds, finally purchasing the estate, then 237 acres, for £19,500. It seems from surviving correspondence between Henry and Caroline that family life at Holland House was contented and relaxed in tone, a place for the family to escape from the demands of politics and the formality of town life. In January 1747, Caroline writes to him 'I like my Country House excessively how glad I should be to have you here with me'.[50] And later the same month '... the country Air does agree very much with me you can't imagine how well I am here to what I am in London, or Bath...I almost always breakfast at home; and walk in the fields up to the knees in dirt for an hour or two after. The weather is delightful now the frost has gone...'[51] And a year later: 'we must have two cows at HH all summer long else we shall not have plenty of good cream which is my delight'.[52]

THE WILDERNESS STARTS TO DISAPPEAR BUT THE WATER GARDEN SURVIVES

There are two surviving surveys from this period, one of the parish of Kensington dated 1766[53] and the other a much more useful – and probably more accurate – estate survey of 1770.[54] Together with other evidence, these capture the changes made by Henry Fox, and the earlier features that still survived. The Wilderness with its eight *allées* so crisply delineated in the 1694/5 survey starts to look a little more ragged, probably partly through neglect but also because by mid-century its formality was rather old-fashioned and not in keeping with the style of planting Fox undertook elsewhere in the park. A survey by Rocque made between 1741 and 1745 shows the Wilderness and the contour of the hill on which it sits (Fig. 13). Only six allées remain and on the east side the space between three allées is now filled with trees and undergrowth, probably self-seeded. In the Vardy drawing of Holland House, 1752 (Fig. 17) the straight lines of the Wilderness can still be seen in the background. The Rhodes survey of 1766 also shows six remaining allées, scattered trees indicating the position of the other two and the enclosing hedge has gone (Fig 14).[55] By the time of the estate survey of 1770 (Fig. 15), only four recognisable *allées* and the remains of a fifth have survived, with individual trees (perhaps left from clearance or planted) occupying the clearings.

Down to the south west the 1770 survey shows that the old water gardens had survived almost unchanged (Fig. 16). '32' is 'Mr Machines Mote [moat] House & Ponds' (Mr Machine would have been a tenant of the estate) and the area is given as just over 4 acres. The enclosing canal seems to have

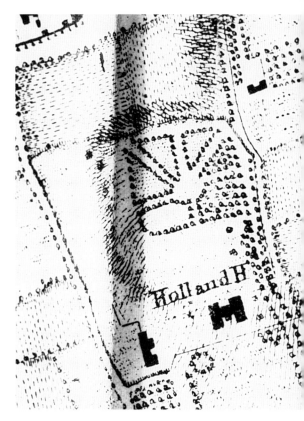

13. Detail from John Rocque's survey published in 1746, showing the Wilderness, with hatchures to indicate the contours of the land.

14. Detail from Topographical Survey of the parish of Kensington, *Joshua Rhodes, 1766: the Wilderness possibly showing some of the avenues already degraded.*

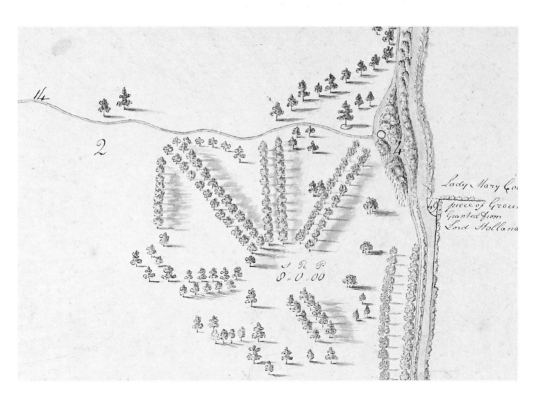

Text on map: *Lady Mary Co...* / *piece of Grou... / Granted from / Lord Holland*

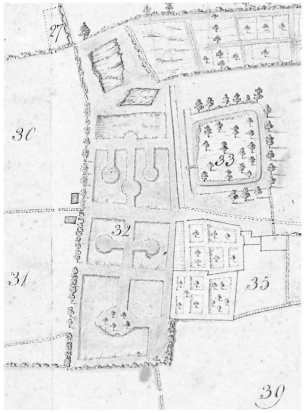

15. *Detail from* An Accurate Survey of the Park, Pleasure Ground and Inclosures adjoining Holland House, *J. Haynes, 1770, showing the wilderness bounded on the north by a path leading to a summer house.*

16. *Detail from* An Accurate Survey of the Park, Pleasure Ground and Inclosures adjoining Holland House, *J. Haynes, 1770, showing the Ponds (32) and the square moat (33).*

been infilled and boundary hedges now run along the west and south sides of the site, following the same line. To the east is the square moat: '33' is 'Orchards belonging to Dᵒ [32]'. It is accessed by a small bridge. Between the moated orchard and the ponds the eastern section of the canal appears to remain. While these older features survived, Fox made dramatic changes to the rest of the pleasure gardens and park.

INS AND OUTS

The old grand approach avenue through Munden Close still appears on Rocque's survey but not on surveys of 1766 and 1770 which show only the eastern (Green Walk) and the western (Holland Lane) approaches. It is reasonable to deduce therefore that it was grubbed up some time after Henry Fox took the property in 1746 and this fits with other changes he made to the access routes. Vardy's drawing of Holland House in 1752 is useful here (Fig. 17).

17. Holland House from the South, *from a drawing by J. Vardy, 1752. Author's annotation.*

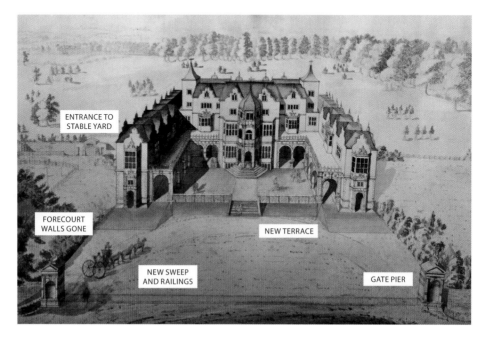

To the west of the house the stable yard can be seen with its north wall. Vardy shows it with a three-arched entrance close to the house: a central arch for carriages, a smaller arch on each side. This implies that by this date at least, there was an access route along the north side of the house, replacing the earlier terrace which was closed by a wall at each end. The drawing also shows that the forecourt walls may have been removed, replaced on the east and west sides by a screen of trees and shrubs. In front a low railing runs between the two gate piers at the corners of the forecourt and a semi-circular sweep allows carriages to approach the centre steps: there must have been a gate at each end of the railing. The inner forecourt has been enclosed by a terrace. This arrangement of the front approach to the house is unchanged in another view dated 1795.[56]

In 1748 a traveller recorded that Henry Fox had added new approaches to the house: 'the present possessor having enclosed the park, and made a coach road into Acton Road, and a coach-way through his own grounds from the turnpike to the house'.[57] The coach-way from the Kensington turnpike followed approximately the line of the present Holland Walk (which was only separated from the rest of the estate and made a public footpath in 1848). It is likely that Fox had a new entrance made here to avoid the constant payment of turnpike tolls when going to and from London (Fig. 18).

18. *The entrance from the Kensington turnpike.* Detail from An Accurate Survey of the Park, Pleasure Ground and Inclosures adjoining Holland House, *J. Haynes 1770. Author's annotation.*

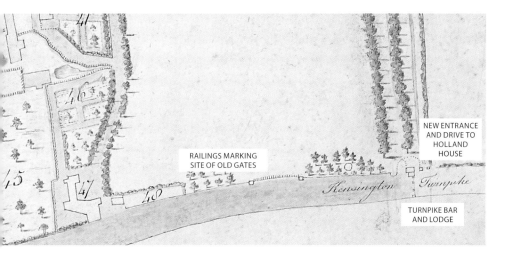

19. Elevation showing the entrance gates to the right of the turnpike lodge. Detail from Plan of Roads under Kensington Turnpike Trust, *Salway, 1811.*

The 'Plan of Roads under the Kensington Turnpike Trust', dated 1811, is accompanied by drawings of the elevations of buildings along the road. One section (Fig. 19) shows the west end of Phillimore Place , then the entrance gates to Holland House and next to that the turnpike toll house. Continuing west, the wall gives way to railings (where the earlier entrance gates stood) through which Holland House can be seen on its rise (Fig. 20). In 1820 this iron fence 'which opened a view of the house to travellers' had been 'lately removed, and replaced by a wall; and a small flourishing plantation promises soon to shut up the new row of brick buildings on the opposite side of the road, which disfigure, though they do not intercept, the prospect from the house'.[58]

The access road north to the 'Acton Road' (now Holland Park Avenue) was made around 1751 when Fox acquired a strip of land from his neighbour Mr Phillimore. It seems by doing this he enclosed a footpath but provided an alternative route '[I] have put my pale on the other side of the hedge, and have made a walk for the Kensington people, which reconciles them to me'.[59] The walk he created was probably the northern end of what is now Holland Walk. An access route from the north which turned a right-angle

20. *Holland House seen through the railings shown on Fig 18. Detail from* Plan of Roads under Kensington Turnpike Trust, *Salway, 1811.*

to run along the north front of the house and into the stable yard matches the Vardy view and the 1770 survey (Fig. 21). This survey also shows the sweep in the forecourt and the railings between the gate piers. South of the railings a semi-circle of grass marks the northern end of the old approach avenue, but that has gone and the house is now approached from either the east or west lanes. To the west of the house (7) the stable yard is still dominated by Henry Rich's stable block but most of the old enclosing walls have gone, replaced by hedges and fences.

THE PARK AND PLEASURE GROUNDS

The 1770 survey gives a detailed and naturalistic view of what else has changed in the gardens and park (Fig. 22). The old walled kitchen garden north of the stables has gone, absorbed into a plantation, but there is now a small hedged kitchen garden behind the stables (6). A new, very large kitchen garden has been made in the fields (18) near the ponds. To the east of the house (9) the old, partially walled court has been replaced by a fashionable bowling green enclosed by hedges and a few specimen trees.

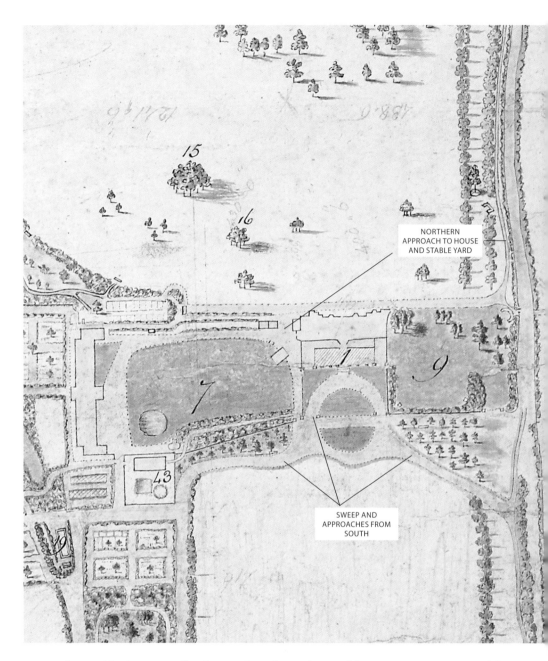

21. The access to Holland House from the north. Detail from An Accurate survey of the Park, Pleasure Ground and Inclosures adjoining Holland House, *J. Haynes 1770. Author's annotation.*

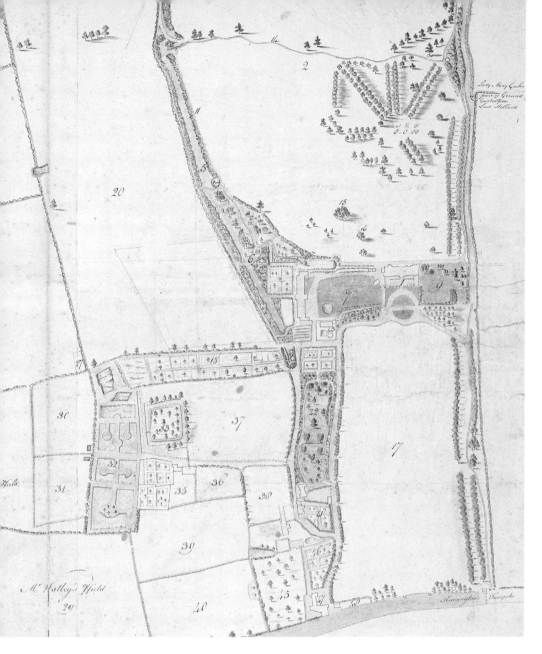

22. An Accurate Survey of the Park, Pleasure Ground and Inclosures adjoining Holland House, *J. Haynes 1770.*

Legend to Fig. 22 (extract)

1. The Mansion House & Courtyard. 5. Plantation & Green Walk. 6. Do. including kitchen garden adjoining to the back of the Stables. 7. Stables, gravel walk, Paddock & Plantation Do. to the IceHouse. 9. Bowling Green. 16. Clump in the Park. 18. Kitchen Garden adjoining Skittle ground. 19. Skittle ground. 32. Mr Machines Mote House & Ponds. 33. Orchards belonging to Do. 42. Miss Gore, little Holland House & garden. 43. Greenhouse & ground belonging [to 42].

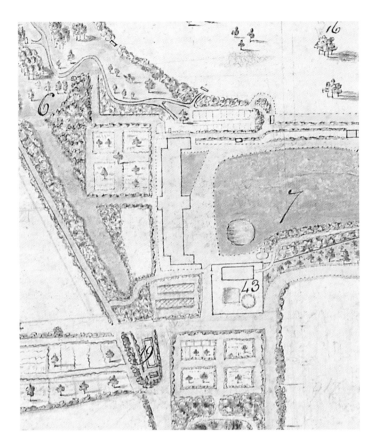

23. The Skittle Ground. Detail from An Accurate Survey of the
Park, Pleasure Ground and Inclosures adjoining Holland House,
J. Haynes 1770.

A bowling green required a lot of maintenance: Charles James Fox (Henry
Fox's younger son) recalled that it was mown every day.[60] South west of
the stables (Fig. 23) an older feature survives: there is a 'Skittle Ground'
(19) on the route to the water garden which may be the 'Bowling Place'
referred to in Sir Walter's will.

The walled gardens, orchards and avenues which in 1695 lay between the
house and the Wilderness have been swept entirely away, replaced by an
expanse of lawn (Charles James said this was mown twice a week) with
scattered clumps and individual specimen trees[61] in the English landscape
style.

DESIGNING THE PARK

Henry Fox admitted that when he began to plant at Holland House he 'did not know an oak from a gooseberry bush'[62] but surviving correspondence shows that he quickly became an enthusiastic and quite knowledgeable plantsman. Lady Caroline, daughter of the Earl of Richmond who created notable gardens at Goodwood, his country estate, was equally enthusiastic.

Fox drew on the advice of Charles Hamilton (1704–1786) of Painshill and Peter Collinson (1694–1768) in designing the planting in the park to achieve the effects he wanted: to create and frame views and to showcase specimen trees. Fox and Hamilton were at Oxford together, stayed in Rome together in 1732 and corresponded regularly over a period from 1741 to 1773 (presumably also earlier, but only letters in this period have survived). Their correspondence is intimate, often teasing:

> My Son of a Bitch of a Coachman forgot to grease the Chaise, tho' I gave him the strictest Charge about it to have it ready, which I fear lost you a Qr of an Hour, and that of yr Time is something.[63]

But Hamilton (who was bankrupted by Painshill) often needed to borrow money from Fox. He was therefore careful always to compliment his friend. When his financial problems were especially fraught in 1756 and he needed help he wrote: 'rambling as my thoughts are, they all point steadily to you as their Center, to you who have ever been the Joy and Comfort of my Life from earliest Youth.'[64]

However in the matter of garden design, Hamilton was invaluable to Fox and he was involved with the gardens at Holland House from the early 1750s. He knew how to manipulate scenery: at Painshill he created the illusion of the grounds being larger than they were and although there was less scope at Holland House, his hand can be seen in the effect remarked on by Elizabeth Montague in 1765: 'There is an air of grandeur in it beyond what the extent should seem to allow'.[65] In 1820 much of his planting was still flourishing: '[Hamilton] introduced several American trees and a vast variety of curious oaks…The cedars planted under his direction are much admired and one clump in particular, situated to the north west, affords with its dark branches, a fine frame to the prospect, and the setting sun in a summer evening'.[66] When this clump was planted the ground was reportedly manured with the covers of old letters.[67] Hamilton planted exotics from America at Painshill and he particularly admired American oaks.[68]

Peter Collinson was an English Quaker cloth merchant and naturalist: his trade with the American colonies enabled him to enlist collectors to send him plants and seeds. He supplied these new and exotic imports to his many horticultural friends and wealthy garden makers.[69] He supplied both Fox and Hamilton and from 1750 to 1756 at least he joined Hamilton in advising on the planting at Holland House. Although this friendship was younger than Fox's with Hamilton, the tone quickly became intimate, from 'Friend Collinson' to 'My Dear Friend' and 'Dear Friend Peter'. They corresponded about politics as well as plants and Fox drew on Collinson's knowledge of and contacts in North America where Britain was clashing with France over colonial territories.

Hamilton and Collinson, who shared an enthusiasm for North American trees and plants, were often invited to Holland House together for consultations over a period of at least six years when most of the re-landscaping at Holland House must have been carried out. On 18 December 1750, Fox wrote to Collinson: 'Friend Hamilton can not come here on Thursday but says it will be as agreeable to you to meet him & to dine here with Him on Saturday which pleasure Lady Caroline & I expect with great impatience. May I beg you to call on Mr. Hamilton & make him come early on Saturday for he has a great deal to do. And if you will permit us, Lady Caroline has a thousand Questions to ask you about Flowers, & I [not] much fewer about Plants.'[70] Clearly a busy day was planned, perhaps Hamilton walking the grounds to advise on layout while Collinson suggested suitable plants and answered questions. Fox's letters give some idea of what he was planting. In the winter of 1751 he asked Collinson for cones of 'Male Spreading Cypress' (*Cupressus sempivirens*, var. *horizontalis*) for seed as he wanted to raise a good quantity of them. He also wanted acorns of Scarlet Oak (*Quercus coccinea*) and 'a Bushel or more of Chesnuts (*Castanea*) for sowing'.[71]

A postscript to this letter shows that Fox was still learning about plants: 'Mr Watson advised me to sow something with a hard Name, to creep upon the ground and cover with green all the vacant spaces in my young Plantation. I wish you would tell me what it was.' The letter is annotated in a different hand, probably Collinson's: 'Double Snowdrops' and 'To remind him in March to sow Candy Tuft, Rock Stock, Venus' Looking Glass, etc.' These presumably also for ornamenting the ground under young trees in the plantation.

A letter written on New Year's day 1752 shows how their friendship was developing. He wrote to 'thank my Friend for his Letter and kind wishes & wish him very many happy New Years'. He placed an order: 'Is the American Evergreen Oak what I had two plants of from Goodwood under the Name of the Live-Oak? If so, pray procure me the two Pots at a Guinea each pot'. He was right about the name of the Live-Oak (*Quercus sempervirens*). In the same letter he also ordered 'Portugal Cypress (*Cupressus lustitanica*), 'Malta Cypress' (probably the common cypress), and said that he was looking for a good price for a 'Quantity of Pyracanthas' (*Mespilus aculeate*). A local nurseryman was asking 50 shillings a hundred for small plants, 'too great a price to buy thousands at'. The letter ends 'Will you dine here Saturday? You shall be guaranteed home'.[72] In May 1755 he writes: 'You Converse with Conjurers, pray bring me word how many cubick yards of soil will cover an acre of Ground with soil one foot deep'.[73] This suggests he was planning to level and prepare a piece of ground, possibly the new bowling green on the east side of the house, the area of which is given as just over one acre in the 1770 survey.

During the 1750s then, with advice from Hamilton and Collinson, Fox was planting the landscape we see matured in the 1770 survey with cedars, cypresses, American oaks and other exotics (Fig. 22). The open lawns are bordered on the east by an avenue of trees which screens the park from the new access drive from the north. One specimen tree[74] is shown interrupting the walk along the avenue and near it is a seat: the two together probably designed as a focal point. A perimeter path gave opportunities for exercise within the park. A gravel walk (11) is shown starting just north of the stable block, running north west, past a pond and alongside a hedgerow before turning east across the open park, north of the wilderness, offering a variety of views out over the countryside. This walk is identified in the survey as 'cross gravel walk to the thatch'd House', which was probably a summer house (Fig. 15). From there the gravel walk continued down the outside of the avenue and returned to the north front of the house.

THE GREEN WALK

On the west the most striking feature of the redesigned park is the plantation north of the stables and kitchen garden and the Green Walk[75] which runs north west almost to the boundary of the estate. Originally a lane through the estate, Fox had it closed off[76] and Charles Hamilton advised on the planting of it. The estate fields to the west of the Green Walk did not form part of the pleasure grounds and were let to various tenants. The line of the Green Walk is now covered by Abbotsbury Road. It is not clear when the Walk was planted: a survey of 1766 appears to show the lane before work began (Fig. 24). But the 1770 survey must show the Walk after Fox implemented Hamilton's advice on how to embellish it and incorporate it into the pleasure grounds (Fig. 25).

A green and shady walk had long been part of the garden repertoire, recommended to begin close to the house so that 'thereby you may enter into immediate Shade, as soon as out of the House, without being heated by the scorching Rays of the Sun'.[77] In the previous century the shade would have been provided by straight tunnel arbors of trelliswork with hornbeam, vines or other climbing plants trained over them. By the mid-eighteenth century the style was trending more towards the natural and picturesque, bringing the countryside into the scope of the garden, a trend which was exemplified by the *ferme ornée*: a working farm (or sometimes more what we might now call a hobby farm) which was enhanced for enjoyment with paths laid alongside hedgerows made ornamental with the addition of mixed shrubs and herbaceous plants.[78] This was an idea first voiced by Addison in 1711:

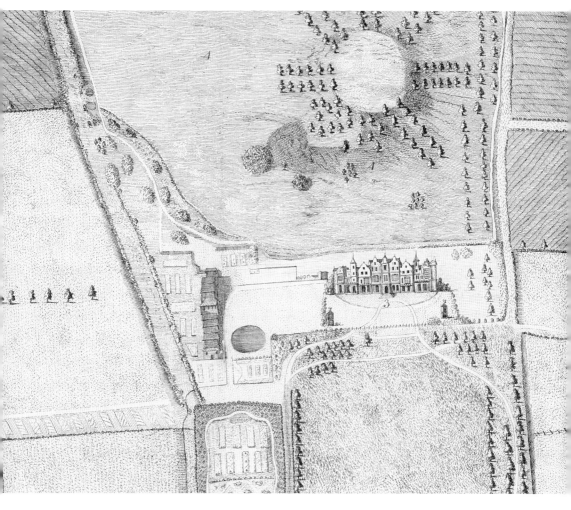

24. The southern section of the Green Walk, possibly before it was ornamented, running north-west from behind the stable block with kitchen garden behind. Detail from Topographical Survey of the parish of Kensington, *Joshua Rhodes, 1766.*

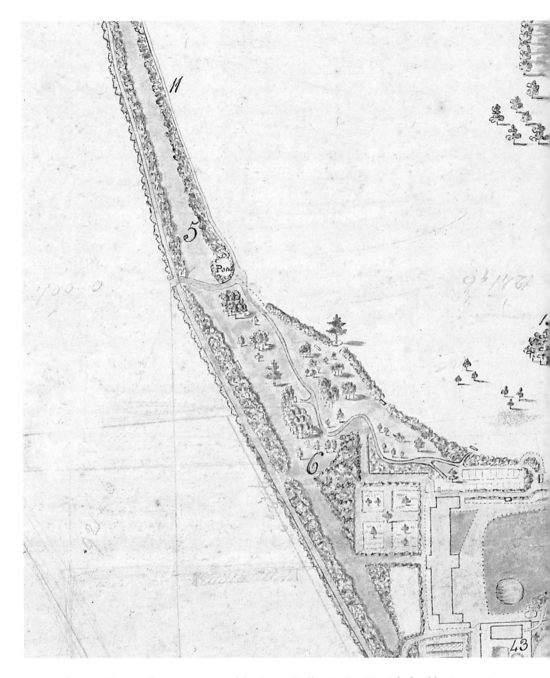

25. Showing the same section of the Green Walk as in Fig. 24, with shrubberies, specimen trees and other ornamental planting. Detail from An accurate survey of the Park, Pleasure Grounds & Inclosures adjoining to Holland House in the County of Middlesex. Surveyed 1770, *J. Haynes.*

'Fields of corn make a pleasant Prospect, and if the Walks were a little taken care of that lie between them, if the natural Embroidery of the Meadows were helpt and improved by some small Additions of Art, and the several Rows of Hedges set off by Trees and Flowers, that the Soil is capable of receiving, a Man might make a pretty Landskip of his own Possessions.'[79]

It is pleasing that some forty years later, Charles Hamilton designed a green walk in Addison's spirit at Holland House. The green and shady walk, turfed for comfortable strolling, would have been a pleasing contrast on the one side to the open park which would be glimpsed through carefully placed gaps in the planting, and on the other sheltered from, but offering glimpses of, the working fields. As the walk was created from an existing lane there would have been established hedgerows but it would have been ornamented with extra planting. Instructions for such planting were very specific, for example:

'The most beautiful Forest-Trees for Hedges are the *English* Elm, the *Dutch* Elm, the Lime-Tree and the Hornbeam. Trees of the shady walks & groves [should] be planted with Sweet-Brier, White Jessamine [jasmine] and Honey-Suckles, environ'd at Bottom with a small circle of Dwarf-Stock, Candy-Tuft, and Pinks.[80] The Hedge-Rows of the Walks be intermix'd with Cherries, Plumbs, Apples, Pears, Bruxel Apricots, Figs, Gooseberries, Currants, Raspberries, etc, and the borders planted with Strawberries, Violets etc.'[81]

Such walks were designed to engage all the senses and this one was recalled with pleasure by Charles James Fox: '[he] shewed me a green Lane or avenue which his mother, the late Lady Holland, had made by shutting up a road. He was a very exquisite judge of the picturesque and had mentioned to me how beautiful this road had become since converted to an alley'.[82] It is interesting that he attributes the Green Walk to his mother: Caroline Lennox spent more time at Holland House than her husband and she and her sister Sarah Lennox (who also spent time there) did garden.

Using the 1770 survey (Fig. 25) we can take a walk through 'this verdant glade [which] would have satisfied the fancy of Spencer, when composing his Fairy Queen *(sic)*'.[83] The walk is divided half way along its length by a crossing gravel path and in the angle formed by the paths a pond is shown. To the north of this crossing path the walk narrows, bordered on each side by hedgerows of (the drawing suggests) mixed species. The southern, triangular area of the walk is more interesting, here the walk widens out to encompass open glades, shrubberies (a fairly new concept at that time) and specimen trees. From the corner of the hedged kitchen garden the old lane runs between a deeper hedgerow of mixed planting and a triangular shrubbery. Emerging from the shrubbery, the view widens out to an open grassy glade dotted with clumps and individual trees. On the other side of the kitchen garden the gravel walk describes a lazy curve to run through the centre of the glade on its way to the pond. A curving hedge divides the glade from the park, emphasising its enclosed and secluded feel. The whole is carefully designed with view points marked by seats along the way. One seat punctuates the park hedge, giving views out into the park; another is at the mid point of the curving gravel walk, backed by a semicircle of trees; a little further on another sits against the outer hedgerow with a magnificent specimen tree as its focal point. This tree and another of the same shape nearer that seat are clearly shown as the largest trees in the plantation: they look like cedars, although Faulkner says that near the 'southern entrance' to the Green Walk 'are two noble oriental planes, remarkable for the size they have attained in this climate'.[84] A 1770 description of Hamilton's planting at Painshill perhaps gives us an image for Holland House: 'the thickets are of flowering shrubs; and the openings are embellished with little airy groupes of the most elegant trees, skirting or crossing the glades'.[85]

The 1770 survey shows the mature landscape created by Henry Fox and his advisers Hamilton and Collinson over the previous twenty years. The high period of the English landscape garden was between about 1730 and 1760 and the gardens at Holland House reflected many of its desirable features:

> In a fine extensive garden or park, an Englishman expects to see a number of groves and glades, intermixed with an agreeable negligence, which seems to be the effect of nature or accident. He looks for shady walks encrusted with gravel; for open lawns covered with verdure as smooth as velvet...[86]

In the last years of his life Fox developed an interest in gothic architecture and was absorbed in constructing numerous gothic 'ruins' at his seaside retreat, Kingsgate, on the Kent coast.[87] He had two surviving sons, Stephen (the heir) and Charles James Fox. But Henry, his wife and Stephen died within a year of each other in 1773/4 leaving Stephen's son Henry Richard, as the one-year-old heir. Mother and son left Kensington and for the next twenty years the house and lands were let to various tenants. Little would have changed in the gardens at Holland House until Henry Richard, the 3rd Lord Holland returned from his Grand Tour and married in 1796.

1796–1874
'ITALIANATE' DESIGNS AND A RETURN TO FORMALITY

T HE PREVIOUS CHAPTER DESCRIBED the gardens created by Henry Fox as shown in the survey of 1770 but the plan is also inscribed 'Estate about Holland House 1770–1796' so it is reasonable to assume that the gardens were largely unchanged during that period. They lay quiet until 1796 when Henry Richard (1773–1840) took possession of his estate. While travelling in Europe he had met Elizabeth Webster (née Vassall) and the relationship resulted in a sensational divorce. She had several children from her first marriage and was pregnant by Henry Richard Fox when they married in 1797.[88] Despite the social stigma attached to divorce, Lady Holland became famed as a social and political hostess and her 'Dinner Books', recording those who dined at Holland House over a period of forty years, are a catalogue of the leading politicians, writers, poets, actors and artists of the day.

The couple spent lavishly on their lifestyle, renovating the house and remodelling the gardens to create a suitable setting for their social life: the focus of the garden now shifted to areas close to the house where sweeping changes created new environments for entertaining. The gardens created then will be recognisable to today's visitors. The first casualty was Henry Rich's magnificent stable block, which after 170 years of use may have been rather dilapidated. More likely it was now felt to be too close to the house, the space needed for other uses. It was partially demolished in 1812, leaving an exposed section of brick arches, five of which still stand: 'the stalls were within lofty arches, which have been preserved, and present something similar to the ruins of an aqueduct, which has a remarkably good effect'.[89] They were clad with ivy for a picturesque effect. The southern portion of the building was converted into a conservatory with an assembly room at its northern end. A new stable block with stalls, two double coach houses, a single coach house and various workshops was built around a courtyard a little down the slope to the south east, so less visible from the house, and these buildings survive. They are seen on the Metropolitan Sewers Survey maps covering Kensington which were produced in 1851 (Fig. 26).[90]

Demolition of the old stables meant that Henry Fox's access route along the north front of the house was no longer needed and a terrace was laid. The area of the old stable yard, described in the 1770 survey as 'Stables, gravel walk, Paddock & Plantation to the Ice House' was laid out in a series of formal gardens with a terrace along the north side, ornamented with vases, and backed by a (probably) older brick wall.[91] By 1851 there were two Ice Houses: perhaps more capacity was needed to meet the demands of the Hollands' lavish hospitality (Fig. 27). The pond (which had supplied water to the old stables) is by no means large enough itself to produce sufficient ice in winter: supplies may have been carted from the 'Moats' or further afield.

The old stable yard was divided by hedges and gravel paths into compartments and formal parterres. A description of 1820 mentions a circular rosary and a 'parterre laid out in various scrolls and devices in the Italian style'.[92] Italian gardens would have been familiar to the 3rd Baron and his wife and this one was originally laid out in 1812. It is attributed to Buonaiuti, factotum to the Hollands. Serafino Buonaiuti started his London life at the end of the eighteenth century as an opera librettist but also earned a living translating and publishing Italian books, then in demand: in 1796 he collaborated in producing a five volume anthology of Italian literature. In the early 1800s he entered the service of the Hollands and soon made himself invaluable. As well as laying out the 1812 garden, Buonaiuti taught the children Italian, supervised repairs, worked in the library and generally took charge at Holland House when the Hollands were away.[93] Lord Holland and his wife both spoke Italian,

26. The new stables and courtyard built c. 1812. Detail from Metropolitan Sewers Survey, *central Kensington, 1851, sheet 494SE.*

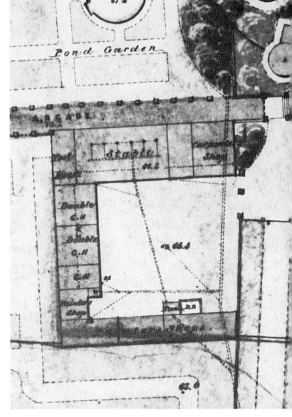

27. The Pond Garden and the two Ice Wells. To the south is part of the arcade built in 1848 to link the conservatory and assembly room to the house. Detail from Metropolitan Sewers Survey, *central Kensington, 1851, sheet 494SE.*

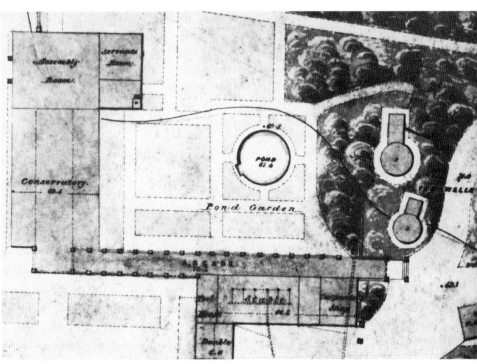

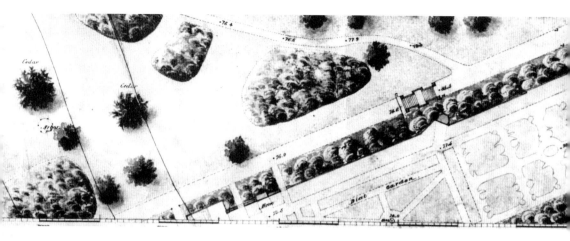

28. Showing part of the formal garden on the west front of the house. Detail from
Metropolitan Sewers Survey, central Kensington, *1851, sheet 494SW.*

decorated their home in the Italian style and Holland House hosted many
eminent Italian visitors. Creating an Italian garden was a declaration of
their interests and sympathies. Lord Holland described it: 'There is a
fountain, with old marble columns in the middle, and black borders and
green figures, and all sorts of gimcracks'.[94] The 'gimcracks' may have been
fragments of Italian marbles acquired on their travels, 'green figures' may
refer to topiary (considered characteristic of Italian gardens) but the
'black borders' are a bit of a mystery. The 1851 survey (Fig. 28) shows part
of these formal gardens enclosed on the north by the terrace, with a deep
shrub border and a wall behind. On the left is the Dial Garden, with a
sundial at its centre. Between the two layouts, on the terrace, is an angled
'Arbour' which visitors today will recognise as the Aedicule with its ogee
arch and wooden seating. Between these parterres and the 'Ivy Arches'
another small garden enclosed by box hedges had a fountain in the centre
and at the south end 'on a column of Scotch granite, 6 feet 10" high, is
placed a bronze bust of General Buonaparte, by Canova, taken at the time
he was Commander in Chief of the Army in Italy: it is esteemed a fine
specimen of the work [of Canova]' (Fig. 29).[95]

Napoleon was still on his column in 1937 but it seems he was lost or
mislaid when statuary was put in store after the house was bombed in
1940. The Hollands met Canova in Rome in the winter of 1814 during a

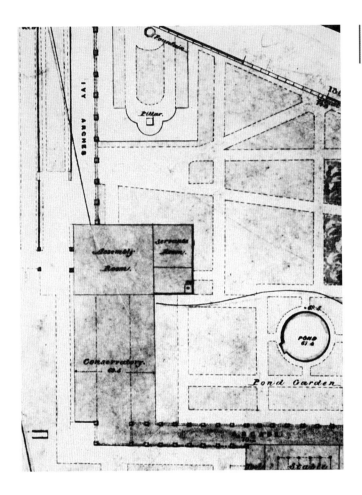

29. *The small garden enclosed on one side by the 'Ivy Arches', with a hedged exedra for the 'Pillar' carrying Napoleon's bust, facing a fountain. (The diagonal line behind the fountain is the edge of this map sheet). Detail from* Metropolitan Sewers Survey, central Kensington, 1851, sheet 494SE.

one year tour and may have purchased or commissioned the work then. It is uncertain whether the bust was by Canova himself but it certainly was of his studio: in September 1815 Lady Holland wrote to Canova: 'several days after our return your beautiful bust of Napoleon arrived, and we are now thinking of selecting a place to preserve for ever the memory of the great Hero, and of the no less great sculptor who cast it'.[96] Lord Holland had a plaque attached:

> He is not dead, he breathes the air
> In lands beyond the deep,
> Some distant sea-girt island, where
> Harsh men the hero keep.

58

The lines are from Homer's *Odyssey*[97] but the reference is to the island of Saint Helena in the south Atlantic where Napoleon was imprisoned by the British and where he died in 1821. Holland's European sympathies may have been fostered by his time abroad: at all events it seems that for a time Holland House became a centre of English Napoleonism.[98]

Facing Napoleon, and behind the fountain, an alcove in the terrace wall was originally a fireplace in a wash house at the north end of the old stable block, a room for drying tack and making equine medicines.[99] The fireplace has survived and is known today as 'Roger's Seat' having been inscribed with a 'distich in honour of Samuel Rogers Esq' composed by Lord Holland in 1812:

> Here Rogers sat, and here for ever dwell
> With me those Pleasures that he sings so well.

Although little known today, Samuel Rogers (1763–1855), wealthy banker (in his father's bank), poet and dissenter, achieved acclaim in his day 'through critical polishing of a minor talent'. But it was the social prestige attached to the circle in which he moved that made everyone seek his acquaintance. Lord Holland would have been part of that circle, especially as Rogers was one of the first connoisseurs of the spoils of Italy with which Napoleon had filled the Louvre.[100] This setting for Roger's Seat and Napoleon was closed on the north by 'a magnificent lofty elm, trunk 15 feet in diameter'.[101] The tree, the ivy clad arches of the old stables, the back of Roger's Seat and the bust of Napoleon on its column are captured in a pencil and ink sketch dated 1817 by John Claude Nattes (Fig. 30).[102]

Lady Holland was credited with being a plantswoman, and although the evidence for that is slim, she is certainly associated with Holland House's role in the introduction of the dahlia to England. In 1789 Vincentes Cervantes, the Director of the Botanic Gardens of Mexico sent seeds of *Dahlia variabilis* to the royal gardens at Madrid. Dahlias were first introduced to England in 1802 by nurseryman John Fraser of Sloane Square, who obtained seeds from Paris of *Dahlia coccinea,* another Mexican species. In May 1804, Lady Holland obtained seeds from botanist Anthony Joseph Cavanilles in Madrid. The cultivation was done by Buonaiuti. However, although plants flowered in a greenhouse they

30. *View of Holland House, Kensington, J C Nattes, 1817. The back of Roger's Seat, Napoleon's bust on its pillar, the ivy-clad arches and in the background, the remaining part of the old stables (the Assembly Room & adjoining Servants Room).*

were afterwards lost, probably though lack of knowledge about how to keep the tubers through the winter.[103] It was not until tubers rather than seeds were obtained from abroad from 1814 on that 'dahlia mania' took off, reaching a peak in the 1830s, echoing the 'tulip mania' of two centuries earlier. Lady Holland's dahlia beds were on the warmer west side of the 'Ivy Arches' until at least 1874 (the area is today a terrace with benches). Dahlia cultivation continued at Holland House (in Napolean's box-hedged garden[104]): in 1901 a list of plants growing in the gardens at Holland House includes 58 different varieties of dahlia.[105]

All the remodelling of the gardens by the Hollands would have needed a lot of labour. The head gardener's account book for 1799–1800 has survived and gives us a glimpse into how the gardens and park were managed.[106] His name was Charles Larkin and he was paid £70 a year. He may have been the only permanent employee as no other gardeners' wages are recorded, but he hired day labourers every week through the year between January and September in 1800, at a weekly cost of between £3 and £4. The wage for a day labourer was probably about two shillings[107]

60

so this represents 30–40 men a week working in the park, orchards and kitchen gardens as well as the pleasure grounds.

Larkin kept separate accounts for disbursements and income for the kitchen garden, park and pleasure grounds. So in 1799 the park costs were £100 0s. 10 ½d. which included a cowman and carter, sheep and sows bought, draining, haymaking, and one guinea for the year to the 'Molecatcher'. In 1800 haymaking on the 'Front park 20 acres' and 'Back park 30 ½ acres' took one month and at the end of June meat, bread, porter and small beer were provided for the harvest home at a cost of just over £16.

Income from the park was a healthy £241 9s. 0 ½d. because produce was costed and charged to the house: 'butter, cream, milk supplied to the House'; 'faggots sent into House' and '6 of My Lord's Horses 13 weeks at grass at 4s.' (four shillings a week). The kitchen garden was equally productive: vegetables and fruit 'sent into House' were charged at £245 6s. 4½d. Larkin has added: 'n.b. the veget^les have been charged very moderately this Year, because it was said they were charged high last Year with a view to swell the Acc^ts.' It sounds as though the housekeeper or steward may have complained! An interesting – and unusual – feature of the accounts is that on one page Larkin has tried to record the qualitative results of expenditure. So, against expenditure of seeds and trees for the Pleasure Ground (£42 2s. 2d.) he has written 'Health'. Against 'Extra jobs, Roads, Walks in HH' (expenditure £150 7s. 4½d.) appears 'Dry Feet'. The annual cycle of production in the park: grazing horses and cows, foraging pigs, haymaking, food and fuel for the house, had probably not changed for two hundred years.

Henry Fox's planting would have been reaching maturity but the park still had an open aspect. Only a few aligned trees remained to show where the Wilderness was, but the Green Walk was still intact. Some of Fox's specimen trees can be identified – at least three cedars in an open glade of the Plantation adjacent to the Green Walk provide a setting for a small arbour (Fig. 31).

On the east boundary of the park the access lane is now identified as 'Lord Holland's Lane' and a deep tree and shrub border separates it from the perimeter gravel walk. An hexagonal summer house is shown and to the south of it, at the intersection of the path with the terrace on the north front of the house, there is a new feature: an apsidal summer house 'containing a colossal statue of the Rt. Hon. J C Fox' (*sic*) The 'colossal statue' was a plaster cast of the statue of Charles James Fox in Bloomsbury Square[108] (Fig. 32).

It is extraordinary that the old 'Moats' survived until the 1820s, but from 1823 plots were sold off for building to finance the lifestyle of Lord and Lady Holland.[109] In 1824 Addison Road was being laid out, the curve of which (where St Barnabas' Church now stands) was dictated by the presence of the ponds. The layout plan submitted to the Westminster

31. Cedars and an arbour on the north lawn. Detail from Metropolitan Sewers Survey, central Kensington, *1851, sheet 494SW.*

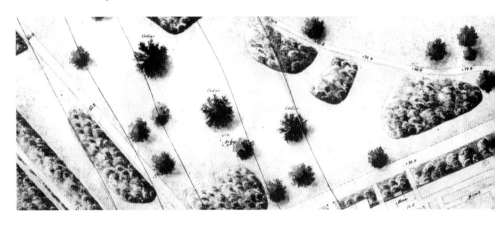

32. The niche for the statue of Charles James Fox. Detail from Metropolitan Sewers Survey, central Kensington, *1851, sheet 495NW.*

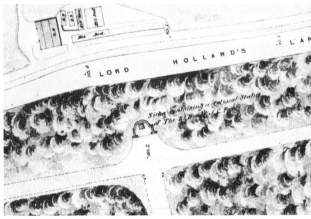

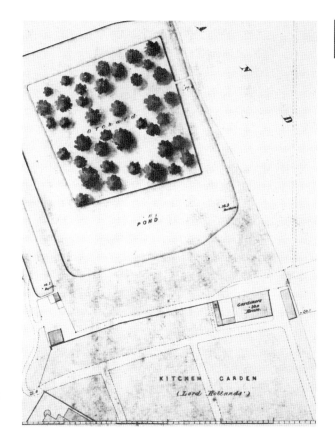

33. *The moated orchard and adjoining 'Kitchen Garden (Lord Holland's)'. Detail from* Metropolitan Sewers Survey, central Kensington, *1851, sheet 494SE.*

Commission of Sewers shows a series of roads avoiding the ponds completely, but no doubt in the course of construction, they were partially or wholly filled in to make one continuous road.[110] The square moated orchard survived longer, shown in 1851 with another kitchen garden laid out south of it (Fig. 33). By 1866 a row of large villas stood on the east side of Addison Road, their gardens covering the ponds' site, but the moated orchard can still be seen (Fig. 34).

In 1840 the 3rd Baron died, leaving the estate to the Dowager Duchess for her lifetime. The estate was now mortgaged, and remained so until well into the twentieth century. An economic recession in the 1820s was followed by a building lull in the 1830s, so development along Addison Road and the two turnpike roads which bounded the estate on the north (Uxbridge Road) and south (now Kensington High Street) had been slow. In the late 1830s some land was lost on the west to the railway linking the

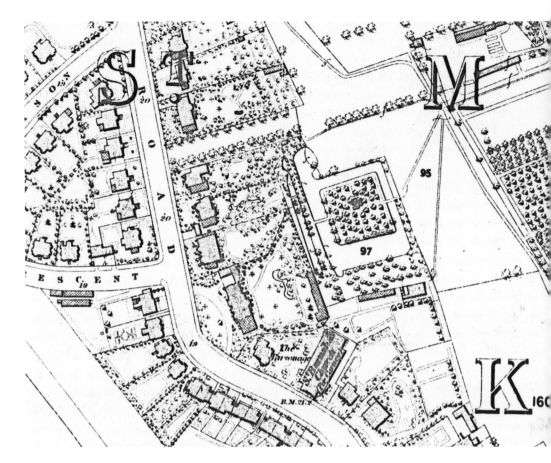

34. *New large villas and St Barnabas church on Addison Road, but the moated orchard (97) still survives. Detail from OS 25" 1st ed., London, sheet 41, surveyed 1866, pub. 1872.*

Kensington Canal with the London & Birmingham railway (now the Olympia branch line). The old Counter's Creek, which had formed the western boundary of the estate was diverted and covered, the line of it laid out as the present Holland Road and Holland Villas Road.

Henry Edward Fox, the 4th and last Lord Holland, was concerned about his mother's plans to sell off further building leases to pay debts and finance her lifestyle. Although much of the land west of Addison Road was still unbuilt on, advisers recommended that land closer to the house would fetch higher prices. In 1845 Henry Edward wrote 'dear old Holland

House must be sacrificed or at least sadly beset by buildings'.[111] In that year the Dowager Duchess died.

Despite his misgivings about the future of the house, the 4th Lord Holland and his wife continued a lavish lifestyle and more land was sold to subsidise them and fund the changes they made to the house and gardens. These changes introduced 'Italianate' design features to the gardens. More accurately this style was 'Anglo-Italian', as 'Italianate' was a later coinage, but it was the height of garden fashion from about 1820 to the 1860s. Those who had travelled in Italy (and many who had not) added features considered to be Italian to their gardens, mostly as hard landscaping: terraces, steps, fountains and statuary. But, some topiary aside, the planting remained completely English. Eventually these gardens became a stylistic mish-mash, variously described as Italian or Dutch or even Portuguese, as the Holland House one was.

In 1848 Lord Holland had the house reoriented for reasons which are unclear, but which may have been linked to a privacy issue. The path running along the south front of the house, and therefore past the entrance, was a public footpath. In exchange for permission to close it Lord Holland gave an alternative right of way, the strip of land which is now the lower portion of Holland Walk. This stirred up local protest: in October 1847 the West London Central Anti-Enclosure Association met to oppose it.[112] One surviving letter of protest was full of scathing 'regret that Lord Holland has no more respect for himself than to do that which his father declared he would not <u>Disgrace</u> himself with, viz, rob the public of their valued footway before Holland House!'[113] On what was formerly the Bowling Green to the east of the house, he now created a new entrance court with the main entrance of the house at the centre of the east front (Fig. 35). On the north wall of the new entrance court the old gate piers were relocated at the top of a divided staircase with a semicircular fountain below, in the Italianate style. The steps created a new access to the higher level of the north garden (Fig. 36).[114] This courtyard on the east front is now occupied by the King George VI Memorial youth hostel.

The material excavated to create the new entrance court was used to build the elevated terrace and arcade along the south front, closing off

STEPS WITH GATE PIERS
GIVE ACCESS TO GARDEN

NEW ENTRANCE

Holland House

ARCADE AND TERRACE LINKING
HOUSE TO CONSERVATORY

NEW TERRACE
CLOSES FORECOURT

Fountain

Fountain

Fountain

Fountain

Lodge

Stables

35. *The new eastern entrance courtyard built in 1848. Detail from OS 1:1056, 1862-5, London sheets 87 & 88. Author's annotation.*

36. *The gate piers and steps giving access from the east courtyard to the gardens. Engraving from Princess Marie Liechenstein,* Holland House *(London: 1874), vol. 1, p. 171.*

what had been the forecourt and sweep and linking the conservatory and assembly room created thirty years earlier to the main house. This was built in two stages as in 1851 the arcade is shown as starting by the Ice House with a flight of steps to access the terrace (Fig. 27). It was completed back to the house in the winter of 1857/8 (Fig. 35). The old assembly room was now remodelled and renamed 'summer ballroom'. An early twentieth century photograph shows the summer ballroom with its turret intended to evoke an Italian loggia and the remaining arches of the old stables, all picturesquely smothered in ivy and other climbers (Fig. 37).

Viewed from the ballroom, the 'Dutch' gardens below were laid out in Italianate style with acute angled geometric beds interspersed with other shapes and filled with mass bedding of a restricted range of plants fashionable from mid-century (Fig. 38). Typically, the bedding (for summer) would have consisted of pelargoniums, petunias, calceolarias, verbenas, salvias and lobelias in a limited range of strong colour combinations. Plants were displayed only when flowering and the effect, instant but temporary, demonstrated the required triumph of art and

38. *The Dutch Garden seen from the Summer Ballroom during a garden party, c. 1894.*

horticultural skill (and money) over nature. In 1883 this style of planting was described 'as near perfection as can well be'[115] but soon it had disappeared from most private estates, labelled 'vulgar' because it had achieved mass popularity, was easily adapted to smaller gardens and was promoted by the popular gardening periodicals. It continued in suburban gardens well into the twentieth century and, in public parks is still with us. We can be certain that during the second half of the nineteenth century, the formal gardens at Holland House would have been filled with combinations of red, yellow and blue flowering plants, greenhouse reared, planted out at their peak by teams of gardeners. In 1874 these gardens were still laid out 'in that good old-fashioned way so rarely met with now'.[116]

But by 1860, when the 4th and last Lord Holland died, half the estate, mainly on the west and north sides (Holland Park and Holland Park Mews) had gone and the remainder was heavily mortgaged. His widow was unable to settle outstanding mortgages or keep pace with her own expenditure. Plans were drawn up for building on the meadow in front of

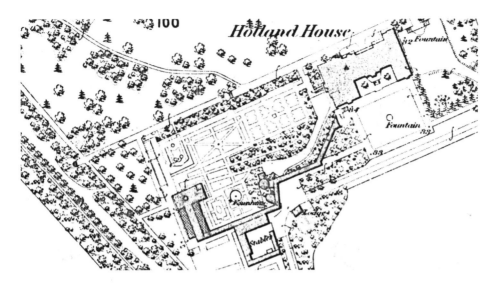

39. *The layout of the formal gardens. Detail from OS 25" 1st ed., London, surveyed 1866, pub. 1872, sheet 41.*

the house but a national financial crisis in 1866 helped forestall this. In 1873 the owner of Oak Lodge on Addison Avenue offered Lady Holland £400,000 for the whole of the estate remaining in her hands, with a view to building on it. Holland Park only exists now because Henry Edward Fox-Strangeways, 5th Earl of Ilchester and descendant of the 1st Lord Holland, agreed to take the mortgaged estate in 1874, in return for allowing the Dowager Duchess to live at Holland House, with an annuity, for the rest of her life.[117] In the same year Princess Leichtenstein (adopted daughter of the Hollands) wrote a book about Holland House and described the gardens: about 80 acres were then left.

From the OS map surveyed in 1866 we can see the layout of the formal gardens which remains almost unchanged today (Fig. 39). The arcaded terrace links the house to the conservatory and summer ballroom. At the south end of the conservatory was a square where orange trees from the conservatory would be displayed in the summer (Fig. 40).[118] The Green Walk running alongside can still be seen but the elegant layout of paths, glades and shrubberies of a hundred years ago has gone. Its rich and varied planting has also gone and it is now described simply as 'like an immense gallery arched with trees and carpeted with grass',[119] but it still gave views over open fields on the left hand, separating it from Addison Road. The OS map shows us what has changed in the rest of the park (Fig. 41).

40. *The area south of the Conservatory where oranges and other tender plants were stood out in summer.* 'Holland House, Kensington, a seat of the Earl of Ilchester', Country Life, *28 February 1903, p. 280.*

The northern part of the estate has been sold and marked out for development but only a few houses have yet been built on Holland Park. An open lawn still lies to the north of the house, sloping up to an old cedar, probably one of Hamilton's plantings, branches often struck by lightning, 'proud of its mutilations'.[120] Other cedars are dotted on the lawn where three summer houses are shown. A straight walk crosses the park and north of it the pond where Lord Holland's statue now stands is shown but only a few scattered trees indicate where the Wilderness was. Lady Holland late in life made her own mark on the park by planting an avenue of lime trees down the western section of this straight path. From the octagonal summer house the perimeter walk which returns to the house was in 1848 renamed in honour of the exiled French king Louis Philippe who visited the house.[121] A sickle shaped belt of woodland almost encloses the northwest corner of the park. What is most noticeable is how open the park still is, when compared with the denser growth of trees that now characterises Holland Park.

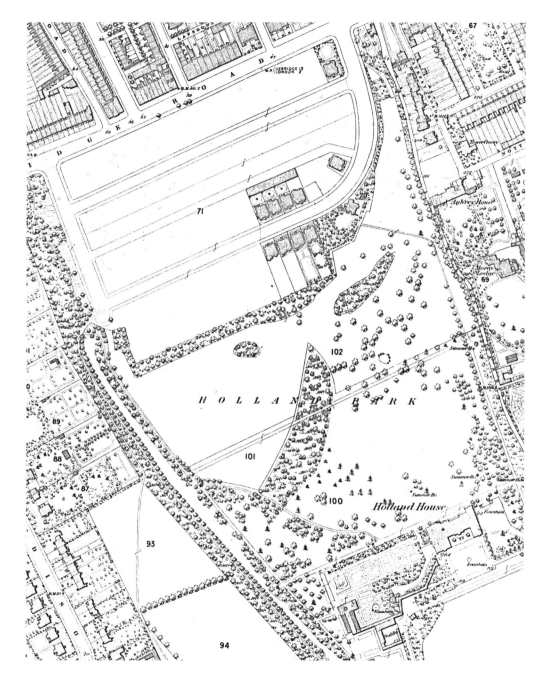

41. The northern part of the estate laid out for building. Detail from OS 25"
1st ed., London, surveyed 1866, pub. 1872, sheet 41.

1874–1940
A PLANTSMAN'S GARDEN

A FTER THE 5TH EARL OF ILCHESTER acquired the estate in 1874 he had to deal with the debts and mortgages but although more land was sold off, happily he prevented building immediately adjacent to the house. His most distinctive additions to the garden in the 1890s were a water and rock garden and a 'Japanese' garden (the present Kyoto garden is the second on the site). The emphasis was once again on planting and the gardens became noted for the variety of plants and some rare introductions. Much of this can be attributed to the skills of Charles Dixon, the Earl of Ilchester's head gardener.

At the turn of the century, on the north front of the house the wide expanse of open lawn still provided a setting for the cedars planted by Henry Fox: in 1877 Lady Holland boasted of fifty cedars outstanding in size and grandeur still standing.[122] But by 1900 those remaining were decaying and in 1937 only three remained.[123] Even before he acquired the estate, Lord Ilchester was funding an extensive planting and restoration programme, including, in 1876, the planting of Lady Holland's Lime Tree Avenue, which stood until the gale of 1987, and was replaced with new lime trees given by The Friends of Holland Park. Many of the now mature trees in the park were his plantings probably including some in the Arboretum and the Oak Enclosure.[124] But it seems some relic trees were still standing in 1899:

> The remains of an ancient orchard forms a feature in the grounds near the house. The gnarled trunks and limbs and quaint contours of the

Apples affording capital contrasts to the stately old Cedars of Lebanon, now getting rather bare, the *Cupressus, Thugas* & Planes.[125]

It is possible that the ancient apples marked the small orchard which flanked the formal parterre, or the adjacent walled kitchen garden, both seen in the 1694/5 survey (Fig. 12). Later orchards were all further away from the house. Beyond the lawn the Rose Garden featured a long grass path bordered by a very popular Victorian rose, the pink 'Mme Caroline Testout', which is still available.[126] Turning left from the top of the Rose Garden the visitor would enter a new garden which must have been a collaboration between the 5th Earl and his head gardener Charles Dixon who was at Holland House until 1919. Dixon was a Fellow of the RHS and in 1901 published a catalogue of all the trees and plants then growing at Holland House.[127] Judging by his wedding photograph he was a vigorous man (Fig. 42). His catalogue together with contemporary descriptions in gardening journals and *Country Life* tell us how the gardens looked around the turn of the century.

The new garden lay in the Oak Enclosure of the present park (not currently accessible to the general public) where there are still three square water tanks constructed of two different colours of bricks (Fig. 43). The tanks are deeper than they appear from the external brickwork and were linked although the connecting channels can no longer be seen (Figs 44 & 45). These were part of a water garden and rockery built in the 1890s but now lost. There was a spring at the highest point of the gardens where the water was collected in a pool 'hidden in a thicket'.[128] From the pool the water was:

Mr. Charles Dixon, aged eighty-two, and his bride, Mrs. Jarrett, aged seventy. Both have been many years in the service of the Dowager Countess of Ilchester, Mr. Dixon being head gardener.

42. *'Mr Charles Dixon, aged eighty-two and his bride, Mrs Jarrett, aged seventy'. Unidentified newspaper cutting pasted into the frontispiece of a copy of Dixon's 1901 catalogue held at the RHS Lindley Library. The wedding must have taken place after 1905 since the cutting refers to the Dowager Countess of Ilchester (the 5th Earl died in 1905).*

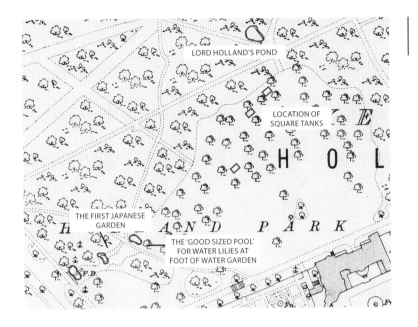

LORD HOLLAND'S POND

LOCATION OF
SQUARE TANKS

THE FIRST JAPANESE
GARDEN

THE 'GOOD SIZED POOL'
FOR WATER LILIES AT
FOOT OF WATER GARDEN

43. 'Plan to show location of the Water Garden tanks and pool and, below that, the first Japanese garden. Based on OS map of 1916 which shows the Japanese garden and the lowest pool of the Water garden, but not the square tanks. Those were described in 1899 (and do appear on later OS maps) so have been added to this plan. Author's annotation.

44. The top tank of the water garden (2011).

45. The second, and, beyond the tree, the third tank (2011).

46. Basin and fountain with water lilies in front of house. 'Holland House, Kensington, a seat of the Earl of Ilchester', Country Life, 28 February 1903, p. 280.

by certain ingenious contrivances led from one part to another on the western side of the great lawn, and supplies, in its course, several square tanks raised above ground level, and trickles in narrow channels lined with pebbles from tank to tank, and the overflow from each runs to one at a lower level and finally reaches a rockery at the boundary of the garden proper.[129]

Moisture from the runnels seeping into the surrounding turf kept the soil moist and the air humid even in the driest periods and provided the perfect environment for moisture-loving plants. The same article describes the planting along the runnels including *Cyperus* (sedges), exotic and native iris, thymes, and bamboos which 'add greatly to the interest of the garden'. The top tank was planted with *Zizania* rice (a wild rice) and the walls with *Dianthus*; the next was also planted with the rice but the walls clothed with a dwarf *Campanula* and *Dianthus* 'Napoleon III'. The third tank was filled with Marliacs Water Lilies and the walls planted with saxifrages. Another tank was filled with *Aponogeton distachyos* (Cape pondweed), so there must have been four tanks although only three can now be seen. The last piece of water, described as 'a good sized pool' was also filled with 'Marliacs Water Lilies' Nymphaea *purpurea*, *N.* 'Marliaca Rosea', *N.* Marliaca carnea, *N. odorata*, and *N. odorata* subspecies *tuberosa*, and around the edges were sedges and various Bamboos.[130] On the south front of the house below the terrace a large stone basin with a fountain was also filled with Marliac water lilies (Fig. 46).

Marliac water lilies were hybrids between the native European white and the colourful tropical and sub-tropical lilies from North America and China that were hardy enough to survive outside in northern Europe. The hybrids were first produced by Joseph Bory Latour-Marliac in south-west France, making a huge impact at the Universal Exhibition in Paris in 1889 and inspiring Monet to add them to his garden – and to paint them.[131] In the 1890s they were among the new plants to have in fashionable gardens so it seems likely that the Holland House tanks were constructed specifically to grow and display them. Charles Dixon's catalogue lists an astonishing 39 varieties of *Nymphaea* growing in the gardens: Marliacs and other hybrids, varieties of the North American *Nymphaea odorata*, the lotus, and other tropical African varieties which must have been kept in a glasshouse. A photograph of 1902 shows one of the water garden tanks with water lilies and the plant-edged channel running from it (Fig. 47).

Below this water garden was a rockery. A photograph of 1899, of perhaps just part of it, shows it as a typical late Victorian construction of piled rocks in a circular bed surrounded by lawn, but alpines seem to have been a speciality of Charles Dixon. They were planted along the watercourses as well as on the rockery and 'a considerable degree of success has attended Mr Dixon's efforts'.[132] The 1901 catalogue lists 61 varieties of saxifrage and 15 of sedum. The challenge of course was to grow alpines in London's coal-fire polluted atmosphere. Mr Dixon was sent a '*Campanula Fosteri' (sic.:* probably *Campanula foersteri*) from the *Jardin d'Acclimatation* in Geneva which was stated to be very unlikely to succeed at Kensington as it needed 'mountain air…yet this purely alpine plant is at this date perfectly healthy and it is making fair growth'. Rather bizarrely, Mr Dixon was also making a trial on part of the rockery of a species of *Opuntia* (prickly pear), noted as 'experimental at this stage'.

47. *The top water garden tank and runnel. 'Holland House, Kensington, a seat of the Earl of Ilchester',* Country Life, *28 February 1903, p. 280.*

Most interesting is the observation that what grows at Kensington ought to do well in London's parks so the gardens were seen as innovative proving grounds at this time.[133]

The Kyoto Japanese Garden in Holland Park, which occupies approximately one acre, was opened in 1991. The Kyoto Chamber of Commerce and the Kyoto Garden Association advised on the design and layout and it was built by a joint British and Japanese team.[134] The first Japanese garden, laid out around 1900 by the 5th Earl of Ilchester would have been inspired by a quite different idea of Japan. After Japan opened its borders to the rest of the world in 1868, a craze for all things Japanese, including gardens, swept Britain. In London, for example, an 'authentic' Japanese Village complete with a small garden was built in Knightsbridge in 1885 (at the top of Sloane Street, near the site of Harvey Nichols). Built by Dutchman Tannaker Buhicrosan who had a Japanese wife and managed a touring Japanese troupe, it presented a kitsch caricature of Japanese life and culture, but prompted a number of imitations across the country.[135] The most renowned early Anglo-Japanese garden was laid out in 1900 at Gunnersbury Park for Baron Leopold de Rothschild. Built north of the Gothick stables, the garden 'had quaint bamboo bridges and summer houses surrounded by native Japanese trees and shrubs'.[136] The water that flowed through a series of concrete-lined channels was heated from the nearby glasshouses so that tender shrubs and fruits could be grown. The rivulets are now dry and all the buildings are lost but some Japanese trees still survive.

So the 5th Earl would have been familiar with this fashionable garden style when he laid out his own Anglo-Japanese garden, extending south west from the rock garden, where steps led down, past a sundial, to a grotto containing a spring. A runnel ran down the slope, crossed by stepping stones, linking a series of pools surrounded by lawns planted with bamboos, yuccas, 'endless varieties of lilies', hydrangeas, roses, chrysanthemums, *Dracaena* varieties and various grasses (Fig. 48).

Towards the bottom of the slope a basin was filled with white water lilies and could be crossed 'in the correct Japanese way by stepping stones, or by a little rustic bridge'.[137] Below that another lawn was planted with 'standard Wistaria,[138] feathery bamboos and the lovely Japanese Iris

48. *The Japanese Garden. A runnel can be seen winding down the slope, edged with grasses, with plantings of yuccas and bamboos around the lawn. Holland House, Kensington, a seat of the Earl of Ilchester'*, Country Life, *28 February 1903, p. 280.*

49. *View of the line of ponds in the Japanese garden. The pool in the foreground is probably the 'good sized pool' shown in Fig. 43. The pool of the present Kyoto garden now covers its site.*

Kaempferi'. The final, lowest basin was filled with rose-coloured *N.* 'Marliaca rosea'.[139] This was an English interpretation of a Japanese garden with an English planting style and lush lawns, the inclusion of some exotics and decorated with a few 'Japanese' touches such as stepping stones and notably the 'old stone lantern, of grey granite, quaintly carved and dating back four hundred years', which can be seen in Fig. 48.[140] This long narrow garden ran below and just to the west of the present Japanese garden (Fig. 49).

The straight edge between the two pools in the middle of the picture may be the 'little rustic bridge' and stepping stones can be seen in the pools. Many of the stepping stones and the smooth stone rim of one of the pools can still be found in the undergrowth which now covers this site (Fig. 50). It is clear from Fig. 49 that the pools were not linked along a central line. Another view shows water flowing over stones in a narrow runnel bordered by sand or gravel, between high planted banks, a distinct

50. Some of the surviving rockwork from the ponds seen in Fig. 49 (2011).

contrast with the smooth lawns around the pools (Fig. 51). Today most of the surviving stone work is on the right of the view in Fig. 49 so the planting on that side may conceal the banked runnel, although there may have been more than one water source to keep the pools topped up. Of the planting in this garden the only survivors seems to be an elderly Katsura tree *(Cercidiphyllum japonicum)* which can be seen in its youth on the left in Fig. 48, a couple of Chusan palms and a quantity of self-propagated bamboo.

From the bottom of the Japanese garden the visitor could turn left back towards the formal gardens behind the house, arriving first at a terraced Italian garden backed by the old stable arches with their curtain of ivy (Fig. 52).

Through the arches the walled and terraced formal garden (now called 'Dutch') remained much as it was laid out in 1812: geometric parterres

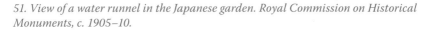

51. View of a water runnel in the Japanese garden. Royal Commission on Historical Monuments, c. 1905–10.

52. *The Italian or 'box garden' Terrace. Through the arch on the left is the bust of Napoleon on his column. 'Holland House, Kensington, a seat of the Earl of Ilchester',* Country Life, *28 February 1903, p. 278.*

edged with clipped box and intersected by narrow gravel paths converging diagonally towards two fountains and an Armillary Sphere placed in a line, some distance apart, in the centre of the garden (Figs 53 & 54). Massed bedding persisted: 'a gorgeous carpet, an intricate blaze of colour'.[141] The dahlias were still being grown in the compartment furthest from the house, enclosed with privet and yew, where Napoleon faced Roger's Seat.

The conservatory at the turn of the century contained a large number of 'aged Camellias, Oranges, Indian Azaleas, Acacias, Oleanders, but it is ill-adapted for the cultivation and preservation [of them]'. There seemed to be few other glasshouses in the garden and those were described as 'of old date, and not very commodious or useful, according to modern

53. Fountain in the Dutch garden. *The planting appears to be massed* Pelargonium. *'Holland House, Kensington, a seat of the Earl of Ilchester'*, Country Life, *28 February 1903, p. 276.*

54. *The Armillary Sphere. 'Holland House, Kensington, a seat of the Earl of Ilchester'*, Country Life, *28 February 1903, p. 279.*

notions'.[142] This observation is surprising as the quantity of non- or just-hardy varieties in the 1901 catalogue suggests the need for extensive glasshouses, but the author had perhaps not seen the nursery area which lay away from the conservatory on the other side of the Green Walk. This screened area had housed a frame yard and hot beds since at least 1850 and by 1916 there was an impressive array of glass (Fig. 55).

Returning from the conservatory to the front of the house along the Italianate arcade (but then called the 'West Cloister') there is a view of the climbers that clothed the whole house: the catalogue contains extensive lists of hederas, wisteria, clematis (56 varieties) and other climbers (Fig. 56). The 1901 catalogue is evidence of a plantsman's garden, with heavy emphasis on flowering trees and shrubs. There are, for example, 236 varieties of Rhododendrons and 16 of Azaleas, 34 decorative pear, apple and sorbus varieties and 45 varieties of *Crateagus* (Hawthorns). The rhododendrons and other ericaceous plants such as *Kalmia* grew on the acidic river gravels which cap parts of the park. 223 varieties of roses are listed: hybrids, tea, pillar, climbing and

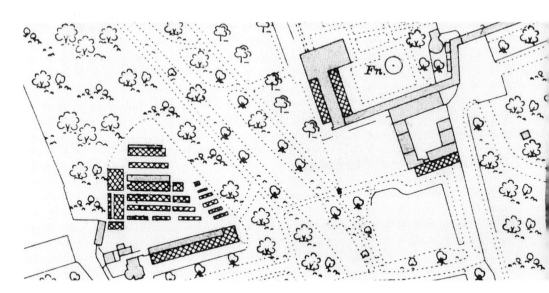

55. *Mr Dixon's extensive rage of glasshouses and frames. The conservatory and stable yard are on the right. OS 1:2500, 1916, sheet IV15.*

56. *'The West Cloister. 'Holland House, Kensington, a seat of the Earl of Ilchester',* Country Life, *28 February 1903, p. 277.*

'other'. There are many autumn flowering perennials but few spring bulbs, which perhaps suggests that the family was absent from the house at that time of year. But there were 15 varieties of *Eucalyptus*, which again shows an interest in exotic introductions. Seven of the woody plants listed were first grown in Britain after 1890 and one, *Broussonetia kazinoki* is still regarded as rare. The trees listed are mainly deciduous, oaks, ashes, acers, all of which would provide wonderful autumn colour; conifers were not in fashion at this time. The catalogue (113 pages and alphabetical) runs from *Abelia floribunda* (an ornamental shrub from Mexico) to *Zizania latifolia* (from NW America: the wild rice grown in one of the water garden tanks).

Considerable tree planting went on throughout the park and the results can be seen in 1916 (Fig. 57). Compare this with 1872 (Fig. 42) when the wooded areas were still concentrated in belts and clumps with a much more open north lawn.[143] Many of the now mature trees in Holland Park date from Lord Ilchester's plantings.[144] Lord Ilchester not only planted, he restored features of the park, most notably the five paths converging on

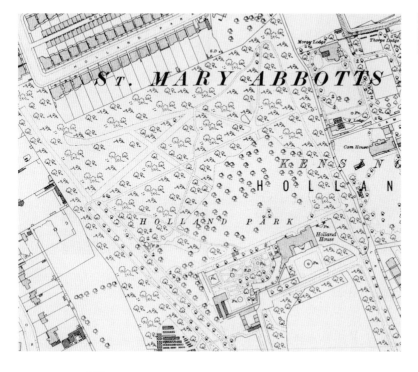

57. *The wooded park in 1916. OS 1:2500, 1916, sheet IV15.*

the pool where Lord Holland's statue stands, raising the ghost of the old Wilderness which occupied this ground. Five *allèes* instead of eight, but the land still falls away to the north and west and if the canopies of the present trees were lifted, there are still views to be seen. What occupies the landscape has changed beyond all recognition in three hundred years but the opportunity to survey the scene beyond the boundaries is something to which everyone still responds.

THE GARDENS JUST BEFORE THE WAR

In 1937 the 6th Earl of Ilchester wrote a history of Holland House, and included a chapter on the grounds past and present.[145] Throughout the gardens, trees were succumbing to old age and storm damage. Of the cedar clump planted by Henry Fox in the mid-eighteenth century on the highest point of the lawn – the north-west corner – only two remained in 1937 (a third still stood nearer the house) and Lord Ilchester feared they would not survive the London smoke much longer. The old beeches which were grouped around the lawn were felled by gales: the finest after a winter storm in 1928. Most of the giant elms, old and decayed, went: Chares Dixon reported eighty trees down after a storm in 1916, and most of those elms. Few of the old elms which had lined the drive up to the house were left, and those which stood along Holland Walk were cut down in the early 1930s because of the danger of falling branches. But the ground on either side of the drive was a mass of bluebells in spring.

The land to the left of the drive, the old meadow stretching down to Kensington High Street was in 1922 laid out as an all-weather golf practice ground, later known rather more grandly as the Kensington Country Club (Fig. 58). It occupied 10 acres: the approach course lay below Holland House, featuring a 250-yard fairway. An eighteen hole putting green, covered tees for all-weather practice and squash courts were laid out to the rear of Melbury Court, screened by trees.

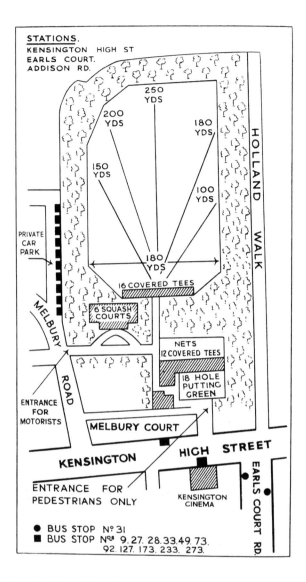

STATIONS.
KENSINGTON HIGH ST
EARLS COURT.
ADDISON RD.

250 YDS

200 YDS

180 YDS

150 YDS

100 YDS

HOLLAND WALK

PRIVATE
CAR
PARK

180 YDS

16 COVERED TEES

6 SQUASH COURTS

MELBURY ROAD

NETS
12 COVERED TEES

18 HOLE
PUTTING
GREEN

ENTRANCE
FOR
MOTORISTS

MELBURY COURT

KENSINGTON   HIGH   STREET

ENTRANCE   FOR
PEDESTRIANS   ONLY

KENSINGTON
CINEMA

EARLS COURT RD.

● BUS STOP № 31
■ BUS STOP №s 9. 27. 28. 33. 49. 73.
            92. 127. 173. 233. 273.

*58. Plan of the golf practice
ground, c. 1922.*

This new development aside, very little had changed in the gardens since early in the century. Behind the house lawns still swept upwards and northwards towards the crest of the hill although Lord Ilchester wrote that the lawns were 'far smaller and more circumscribed fifty years ago (i.e. in 1887) than is now the case' when 'Hayfields took the place of the rose beds, shrubs and trees which now cover the higher slopes'.[146] This is a curious claim, as although the northernmost parts of the estate had probably always been cut for hay, by 1872 that portion of the estate (now covered by Holland Park and adjacent roads) had already been laid out for building. Caroline Testout roses still lined the path from the north lawn to the spot occupied by the statue of Lord Holland. On the highest crest of the hill an old elm tree or two still stood to show where the Wilderness had been. From the top of the rose walk a grass path led south west, past the water garden tanks and flower beds, through scattered trees and shrubs, to the Japanese garden

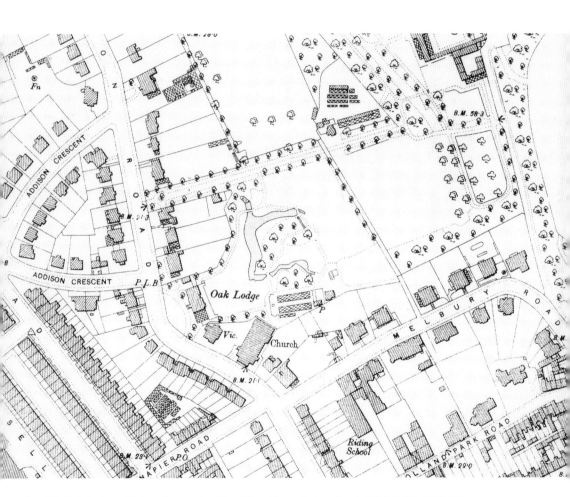

59. Oak Lodge with its lake, on the site of the old moated orchard. OS 1:2500, 1894-96, sheet LXXIII.

planted by the 6th Earl's father. The entrance was masked by high
clumps of rhododendrons and the garden framed by 'plantations and
thickets'. The rockery was still there, planted with alpines, water
trickling from it. The chain of small pools in the Japanese garden was
still flanked by palms, wisteria and magnolia bushes.

The layout of the formal gardens close to the house had hardly changed for ninety years and in 1937 the box-edged geometric beds were brightly patterned with summer bedding. From the south door of the conservatory could be seen the houses of Ilchester Place (built in 1927/8), while to the west, beyond the kitchen garden rose Oakwood Court.

The old moated orchard had been included in a parcel of land sold by Lady Holland in 1871 to a Mr McHenry, who built Oak Lodge and remodelled the square pond into a small English landscape lake fed from the perennial spring and that survived until the last years of the nineteenth century (Fig. 59). The Green Lane had been encroached on by housing at both ends and only a short length remained: most of the elms which marked its position had succumbed to storm damage as elsewhere in the park. The nightingales which gave the lane its popular name had long gone, their last appearance recorded in May 1884 (Fig 60).

Much had been lost, but it is astonishing that, at a time when west London was being rapidly built over, 55 acres of the estate were preserved from development by the Ilchester family. In the inter-war years the gardens at Holland House would have had a mature and tranquil atmosphere. In September 1940 the house was gutted by fire from an incendiary bomb: after the war, the remnant of the old Holland estate entered a new era of its life as a well-loved and valued public park.

ENDNOTES

1   *Mrs Montague, 'Queen of the Blues', Her Letters and Friendships, from 1762 to 1800*, ed. R. Blunt (London: Constable, 1923), Vol. 1, p. 123.

2   Dr Johnson called her a 'very extraordinary person'. A rich woman with great influence and very desirable friends: in her salon she entertained all the leaders of thought and fashion in London.

3   Lyson, *The Environs of London*: Vol. 3: County of Middlesex, 1795, pp. 170–230.

4   See bibliography for publications about the house, its architecture and history.

5   By law, children inheriting property became a ward of the court which appointed a guardian. The guardian was entitled to the income from the estate until the heir came of age, which made them lucrative and much sought-after appointments.

6   Elizabeth Allen, 'Cope, Sir Walter (1553?–1614)', *Oxford Dictionary of National Biography*, Oxford University Press, Sept. 2004; online edn, Jan 2008. [http:// oxforddnb.com/article/6257, accessed 27 May 2010.]

7   John Thorpe built a successful practice in the emerging profession of surveyor, meeting a demand from the crown and aristocracy for accurate estate surveys. He also designed buildings and his manuscript volume of house plans and elevations is now in Sir John Soane's Museum. However, the collection presents problems, in the absence of other documentation, in distinguishing plans which are his original designs from surveys of existing buildings. Malcolm Airs, 'Thorpe, John (1564/5–1655)', *Oxford Dictionary of National Biography*, Oxford University Press, Sept. 2004; online edn, Jan 2008. [http://oxforddnb. com/article/27378, accessed 30 May 2010.]

8   Paula Henderson, *The Tudor House and Garden* (New Haven & London: Yale University Press, 2005), p. 35.

9   '*A Map of part of the Mannors of Earls-Court Kensington & Abbots Kensington in the County of Middlesex being part of the Estate of Edward–Henry Edwardes Esq. Lord of the said Mannors as surveyed Anno. 1694/5 by Edward Bostock Fuller Gent.* Redrawn with an Addition of the Boundaries, Fences, & present Occupiers, July 1734 By D. Johnson & W. Brasier.' The original 1694/5 plan seems not to have survived but the 1734 copy is in the local history archive of the Royal Borough of Kensington & Chelsea.

10 Edward Henry, 4th Earl, died childless in 1721 and the estate passed to the Edwardes family. There is no evidence that any of the family occupied the property: in 1746 they leased it to Henry Fox.

11 Malcolm Airs, 'Inigo Jones, Isaac de Caus and the Stables at Holland House', *The Georgian Group Journal*, vol. XIII, 2003, pp. 141–160.

12 'The Sewer' was Counter's Creek, which marked the western boundary of the estate. It rose near the present site of Kensal Green cemetery and ran roughly south–south-east. The Fulham Road crossed it at a sandy ford (later by a bridge carrying the New King's Road) from where it continued to the Thames as Chelsea Creek, still visible in 1952 as a 'stagnant ditch'. Nicholas Barton, The Lost Rivers of London (London: Leicester University Press, 1962), p. 38.

13 Paula Henderson, *The Tudor House and Garden* (New Haven & London: Yale University Press, 2005), p. 133.

14 Francis Peck, *Desiderata Curiosa* (London: 1732–5), 2 vols: 1, p. 50.

15 Cited in Paula Henderson, *The Tudor House and Garden* (New Haven & London: Yale University Press, 2005), pp. 85, 87, 135.

16 In 1607 King James forced Robert Cecil into giving him Theobolds in exchange for Hatfield.

17 Jennifer Potter, *Strange Blooms, The Curious Lives and Adventures of the John Tradescants* (Atlantic Books: London, 2006), p. 50.

18 The king visited in 1612 but did not stay long as he found the place too cold.

19 Thomas Faulkner, *History and Antiquities of Kensington* (London, 1820), p. 125.

20 Ibid. p. 125.

21 Survey of Westminster, Chelsea & Kensington, 1717. Photographic copy made 1862, National Archives, MPH 1/258.

22 *An exact Survey of the City's of London Westminster, ye Borough of Southwark and the country near ten miles round; begun in 1741 and ended in 1745, by J. Rocque; and engrav'd by R. Parr, 1746; Topographical Survey of the parish of Kensington*, Joshua Rhodes, 1766.

23 M. K. Gloag, *A Book of English Gardens: Holland House* (Methuan, London: 1906), p. 223. The source is not referenced.

24 Paula Henderson, *The Tudor House and Garden* (New Haven & London: Yale University Press, 2005), pp. 132–133.

25 Samuel de Sorbière, *Voyage to England...in 1652* (London: 1708–9), p. 65.

26 Jennifer Potter, *Strange Blooms, The Curious Lives and Adventures of the John Tradescants* (London: Atlantic Books, 2006), p. 37.

27 John Phibbs, 'The persistence of older traditions in eighteenth-century gardening', *Garden History*, 37:2, winter 2009, p. 176.

28 Cited in Giles Stephen Ilchester, 6th Earl of, *Chronicles of Holland House, 1605–1820* (London: John Murray, 1937), p. 8.

29 Trea Martin, *Elizabeth in the Garden* (London: Faber & Faber, 2008), p. 264.

30 Giles Stephen, Ilchester, 6th Earl of, *The House of Holland, 1820–1900* (London: John Murray, 1937), p. 363–4. Sir Walter's original will is at the National Archives, cat.ref. prob/11/125.

31 Ibid., pp. 484–5.

32 It is also possible that they were never installed with gates as originally planned.

33 R. Malcolm Smuts, 'Rich, Henry, first Earl of Holland (bap. 1590, d. 1649)', *Oxford Dictionary of National Biography*, Oxford University Press, Sept 2004; online edn, May 2009. [http://oxforddnb.com/article/23484, accessed 27 May 2010].

34 Malcolm Airs, 'Inigo Jones, Isaac de Caus and the Stables at Holland House', *The Georgian Group Journal*, vol. XIII, 2003, p. 141.

35 This wing was demolished in 1704.

36 Malcolm Airs, 'Inigo Jones, Isaac de Caus and the Stables at Holland House', *The Georgian Group Journal*, vol. XIII, 2003, p. 150.

37 Michael Symes, *A Glossary of Garden History* (Princes Risborough: Shire Books, 2000), p. 132.

38 Paula Henderson, *The Tudor House and Garden* (New Haven & London: Yale University Press, 2005), p. 139.

39 Thomas Faulkner, *History and Antiquities of Kensington* (London: 1820), p. 120.

40 Christopher Morris (ed.), *The Journeys of Celia Fiennes* (London: The Cresset Press, 1947), p. 277.

41 Giles Stephen, Ilchester, 6th Earl of, *The House of Holland, 1820–1900* (John Murray, London: 1937), p. 363.

42 *The Spectator*, No. 474, June 1712.

43 Rogers, Pat, 'Addison, Joseph (1672–1719)', *Oxford Dictionary of National Biography*, Oxford University Press, Sept 2004; online edn, May 2009. [http://oxforddnb.com/article/156, accessed 3 July 2010].

44 *The Spectator*, No. 477, September 1712

45 Jane Fearnley-Whittingstall, *The Garden, An English Love Affair* (London: Weidenfield & Nicholson, 2002), p. 117.

46 At this time Addison was living at Sandy End in Fulham, a short walk across the fields from Holland House.

47 Thomas Faulkner, *History and Antiquities of Kensington* (London: 1820), pp. 76–78.

48 Poet, later Addison's under-secretary, and by publishing a translation of the Iliad in 1714 to rival Alexander Pope's, responsible for a rift between Pope and Addison.

49 Peter Luff, 'Fox, Henry, first Baron Holland of Foxley (1705–1774)', *Oxford Dictionary of National Biography*, Oxford University Press, Sept 2004; online edn, Oct 2005 [http://www.oxforddnb.com/article/10033, accessed 27 May 2010].

50 Holland House Papers, Add. MS 51409, f. 32, British Library.

51 Ibid., Add MS 51409, f. 43, British Library.

52 Ibid., Add MS 51409, f. 113, British Library.

53 *Topographical Survey of the parish of Kensington*, Joshua Rhodes, 1766. Royal Borough of Kensington & Chelsea Local Studies & Archive.

54 *An Accurate Survey of the Park, Pleasure Ground and Inclosures adjoining Holland House*, J. Haynes 1770. British Museum, Crace Collection, port. xxxvi, no. 71.

55 Neither Rocque nor Rhodes was always quite accurate, but the general trend does seem to show a deterioration of the Wilderness.

56 Lyson's, Daniel, *Environs of London*, vol. III, pt.i. p.174, South view of Holland House in Kensington, anon., 1795.

57 Cited in Ilchester, Giles Stephen, 6th Earl of, *The Chronicles of Holland House, 1605–1820* (London: John Murray, 1937), p. 481.

58 Thomas Faulkner, *History and Antiquities of Kensington* (London: 1820), pp. 84–5.

59 Cited in Giles Stephen Ilchester, 6th Earl of, *Chronicles of Holland House, 1605–1820* (London: John Murray, 1937), p. 483.

60 Samuel Rogers, *Recollections, 1763–1855* (pub. posthumously from MS, London: 1859, ed. William Sharpe), p. 55.

61 Specimen trees seem to be identified by being shown with circles round the base of the trunk.

62 From a letter to Lady Hervey, December 1753. Cited in Giles Stephen Ilchester, 6th Earl of, *Chronicles of Holland House, 1605–1820* (London: John Murray, 1937), p. 487.

63 Hamilton to Fox, 2 April 1741, Holland House Papers, Add MS 51408, f. 98.

64 Hamilton to Fox 13 May 1756 Holland House Papers, Add MS 51408, f. 100.

65 *Mrs Montague, 'Queen of the Blues', Her Letters and Friendships, from 1762 to 1800*, ed. R. Blunt (London: Constable, 1923), Vol. 1, p. 123.

66 Thomas Faulkner, *History and Antiquities of Kensington* (London: 1820), p. 121.

67 Giles Stephen Ilchester, 6th Earl of, *Chronicles of Holland House, 1605–1820* (London: John Murray, 1937), p. 489.

68 Michael Symes, 'The Hon. Charles Hamilton at Holland Park', *Garden History*, vol. 3, no. 2, pp. 132.

69 These included Fox's father-in-law the Earl of Richmond, who may have introduced them.

70 Collinson papers, British Library, Add MS 28727, f. 20.

71 Ibid., Add MS 28727, f. 21, British Library.

72 Ibid., Add MS 28727, f. 23, British Library.

73 Ibid., Add MS 28727, f. 38, British Library.

74 In the 1770 survey specimen trees appear to be those shown planted within a circle.

75 Not to be confused with the Green Lane, which ran along the eastern boundary of the estate.

76 There is another path shown along the western boundary which may have been provided as an alternative public footpath.

77 Batty Langley, *New Principles of Gardening*, General Directions, VIII (1728).

78 Geoffrey & Susan Jellicoe, Patrick Goode, Michael Lancaster, *The Oxford Companion to Gardens* (Oxford: Oxford University Press, 1986), p. 186.

79 Joseph Addison, *The Spectator*, No. 37, 12 April 1711.

80 This recalls Collinson's reminder to Fox on what to sow.

81 Batty Langley, *New Principles of Gardening*, General Directions, IX and XiX (1728).

82 Thomas Faulkner, *History and Antiquities of Kensington* (London: 1820), p. 122, quoting from Trotter's Memoirs of Fox.

83 Ibid., p. 121

84 Ibid.

85 Thomas Whately, cited in Penelope Hobhouse, *Plants in Garden History* (Pavilion, London: 1997), p. 200.

86 Tobias Smollett, *Travels through France and Italy, 1766*, ed. Frank Felsenstein (Oxford, 1979), p. 263.

87 Holland House Papers, Add MS 51408 & 51409, British Library.

88 Derek Hudson, *Holland House in Kensington* (London: Peter Davies, 1967), pp. 16–17.

89 Thomas Faulkner, *History and Antiquities of Kensington* (London: 1820), p. 124.

90 The Metropolitan Commission of Sewers was set up in 1847 following epidemics of cholera in London. However it was not until the Metropolitan Board of Works was formed in 1856 with Joseph Bazalgette as Chief Engineer that a comprehensive solution to London's sewerage problems was planned and built.

91 Giles Stephen, Ilchester, 6th Earl of, *Chronicles of Holland House, 1605–1820* (London: John Murray, 1937), p. 491: refers to 'an ancient brick wall'.

92 Thomas Faulkner, *History and Antiquities of Kensington* (London: 1820), p. 122.

93 E. R. P. Vincent, '*Some Italians at Holland House*', MS of a lecture, n.d., Royal Borough of Kensington & Chelsea Local Studies & Archives.

94 Cited in Giles Stephen Ilchester, 6th Earl of, *Chronicles of Holland House, 1605–1820* (London: John Murray, 1937), p. 491.

95 Thomas Faulkner, *History and Antiquities of Kensington* (London: 1820), p. 122.

96 Giles Stephen Ilchester, 6th Earl of, *Chronicles of Holland House, 1605–1820* (London: John Murray, 1937), p. 493.

97 Book 1.1.196.

98 Hudson, Derek, *Holland House in Kensington* (London: Peter Davies, 1967), p. 17.

99 Malcolm Airs, 'Inigo Jones, Isaac de Caus and the Stables at Holland House', *The Georgian Group Journal*, vol. XIII, 2003, p. 144.

100 Richard Garnett, 'Rogers, Samuel (1763–1855)', Rev. Paul Baines, *Oxford Dictionary of National Biography*, Oxford University Press, 2004. [http://www.oxforddnb.com/article/23997, accessed 6 August 2010.]

101 Thomas Faulkner, *History and Antiquities of Kensington* (London: 1820), p. 122.

102 John Claude Nattes was a topographical draftsman and watercolour artist and a founder member of the Society of Painters in Water Colours. At this date he was working in and around London as a drawing master. Aidan Flood, 'Nattes, John Claude (*c*.1765–1839)', *Oxford Dictionary of National Biography*, online edn (May 2007). [http://www.oxforddnb.com/article/19810, accessed 3 May 2009.]

103 J. B. Wroc, *Dahlias and their Cultivation* (London, 1908), p. 9.

104 Giles Stephen, Ilchester, 6th Earl of, *Chronicles of Holland House, 1605–1820* (John Murray, London: 1937), p. 490.

105 Charles Dixon, *Catalogue of Plants growing in the gardens of Holland House, Kensington* (London: Hatchards, 1901), RHS Lindley Library.

106 'Garden, pleasure ground & Park Ledger with Annual Abstracts of [?] Disbursements 1799–1800', MS. 26384 (local), Royal Borough of Kensington & Chelsea Local Studies & Archives.

107 In the accounts a day carpenter, a skilled tradesman, was paid 3*s.* a day.

108 Giles Stephen, Ilchester, 6th Earl of, *Chronicles of Holland House, 1605–1820* (London: John Murray, 1937), p. 485.

109 From 1822 household expenditure annually exceeded the rental income from the farmland on the estate and other properties.

110 'The Holland Estate: To 1874', Survey of London: vol 37: Northern Kensington (1973), pp. 101–126. [http://british-history.ac.uk/report/49870, accessed 18 May 2010.]

111 'The Holland Estate: To 1874', Survey of London volume 37: Northern Kensington (1973), pp. 101–1126.

112 A poster 'Public rights and no surrender' advertised the meeting. Royal Borough of Kensington & Chelsea Local Studies & Archives, cat. C. PIC. 837

113 Letter from Mr Griffiths to Clerk of Clerkenwell Sessions (where the application was to be heard), January 1848. London Metropolitan Archives, cat. MJ/SP/1848/A/049.

114 In 1959 Henry Rich's gate piers were removed from storage and installed in the centre of the south-side terrace at the top of a new flight of steps and hung with gates to gives access to the performance area in front of the old house's façade. Christopher Wood, *H is for Holland, The Sculptures and Architectural Features of Holland Park* (Friends of Holland Park), p. 16.

115 Florist and Pomologist, 1883, p. 146.

116 Princess Marie Liechtenstein, *Holland House* (two vols) (London: Macmillan & Co., 1874), vol. 1, p.175.

117 'The Holland Estate: To 1874', Survey of London volume 37: Northern Kensington (1973), pp. 101–1126.

118 Princess Marie Liechtenstein, *Holland House* (two vols) (London: Macmillan & Co., 1874), vol. 1, p.184.

119 Ibid., vol. 1, p. 191.

120 Ibid., vol. 1, p. 172.

121 Ibid., vol. 1, p. 194.

122 Giles Stephen, Ilchester, 6th Earl of, *Chronicles of Holland House, 1605–1820* (London: John Murray, 1937), p. 490.

123 Ibid., p. 490.

124 *Some Notable Trees of Holland Park, A Walk*, Friends of Holland Park and the Royal Borough of Kensington and Chelsea Ecological Service, 2007, p. 5.

125 *The Gardener's Chronicle*, vol. 25: 1899, pp. 267–8

126 In 1904 one bed at Gunnersbury Park held 'over 500 plants of Caroline Testout'. *The Gardener's Chronicle*, vol. 36, 1904, p. 26.

127 Charles Dixon, *Catalogue of Plants growing in the gardens of Holland House, Kensington* (London: Hatchards, 1901). These 'what's growing in my garden' publications usually bore the name of the landowner or the professional horticulturalist who did the job and this catalogue demonstrates very good record keeping at Holland House.

128 There were several springs on the estate: the one feeding the Moats has been mentioned before. They rose where patches of river gravel lie above impermeable London clay. As the Thames valley aquifer has been much depleted over the past century the springs have ceased to flow, making their presence felt only as frequent patches of muddy ground. One appears regularly near the gate to the Oak Enclosure, close to the top tank. The water supply in the park now is supplied by a bore-hole sited at the top of the Kyoto Garden.

129 *The Gardener's Chronicle*, vol. 25: 1899, pp. 267–8

130 Ibid., pp. 267–8

131 *The Garden*, January 2011, pp. 44–47

132 *The Gardener's Chronicle*, vol. 25: 1899, p. 269

133 Ibid., p. 268

134 *The Kyoto Garden in Holland Park*, Friends of Holland Park, 1991.

135 Joanna Pitman, 'Some of London's Japanese gardens', *London Gardener*, vol. iv (1998–99), p. 33.

136 *The Gardener's Chronicle*, vol. 36, 1904.

137 M. K. Gloag, *A Book of English Gardens: Holland House* (London: Methuan, 1906), pp. 232–233.

138 'Wistaria' is the correct, original spelling.

139 M. K. Gloag, *A Book of English Gardens: Holland House* (London: Methuan, 1906), p. 234.

140 Ibid., pp. 233–234.

141 Ibid., p. 237

142 *The Gardener's Chronicle*, vol. 25: 1899, p. 268

143 By 1940 the cover was more complete and after the neglect of the war and postwar years there was a huge clearance job to be done in grubbing out dense growths of self-seeded Sycamores and Robinias.

144 *Some Notable Trees of Holland Park*, Friends of Holland Park, 2007.

145 Ilchester, Giles Stephen, 6th Earl of, *Chronicles of Holland House, 1605–1820* (London: John Murray, 1937), Ch. XVII, pp 481–507.

146 Ibid., pp. 485–6.

Bibliography

Unpublished sources

Correspondence of 1st Lord Holland, Holland House papers, British Library, Add MS 51408 & 51409.

Correspondence of Peter Collinson: Collinson papers, British Library, Add MS 28727.

Garden, pleasure ground & Park Ledger with Annual Abstracts of [?] Disbursements 1799–1800. MS 26384 (local), Royal Borough of Kensington & Chelsea Local Studies & Archive.

Letter from Mr Griffiths to Clerk of Clerkenwell Sessions, January 1848, London Metropolitan Archives, cat. MJ/SP/1848/A/O49.

Maps and Plans in date order

A Mapp of part of the Mannors of Earls Court Kensington and Abbotts Kensington in the County of Middlesex being part of ye Estates of Edward-Henry Edwards esq., Lord of the said Mannors, Surveyed anno 1694/5 by Edward Bostock Fuller, gent. Redrawn with an Addition of the Boundaries, Fences & present Occupiers, July anno 1734 by J. Johnson and W. Brasier.

Royal Borough of Kensington & Chelsea Local Studies & Archives .

Survey of Westminster, Chelsea and Kensington, 1717 (photographic copy made in 1862). National Archives, cat. MPH1/258.

An exact Survey of the City's of London Westminster, ye Borough of Southwark and the country near ten miles round; begun in 1741 and ended in 1745, by J. Rocque; and engrav'd by R. Parr, 1746.

Topographical Survey of the parish of Kensington, Joshua Rhodes, 1766.

Royal Borough of Kensington & Chelsea Local Studies & Archives.

An Accurate Survey of the Park, Pleasure Ground and Inclosures adjoining Holland House. J. Haynes, 1770. British Museum, Crace Collection, port. xxxvi, no. 71.

Holland House with Adjacent Grounds, December 1796. British Museum, Crace Collection, port. xxxvi, no. 72.

Plan of Roads under the Kensington Turnpike Trust, Salway, 1811, Sheet 2.

Royal Borough of Kensington & Chelsea Local Studies & Archives .

Elevations as shown of Roads under the Kensington Turnpike Trust, 1811.

British Museum, MS. 11075.

Metropolitan Sewers Survey, 1851, central Kensington, sheets 467SE, 494SE, 494SW, 495NW, 522NW. Royal Borough of Kensington & Chelsea Local Studies & Archives .

Ordnance Survey:

1:10000 (6"): skeleton sheets for 1st edition, 1848–1850, London and Environs, sheet VI.S.E.

1:1056 (5ft.): 1862–65, London sheets VI87 & VI88.

1:1056 (5ft.): LCC revision, 1940, vol. 46.

1:2500 (25"): 1st edition, surveyed 1866, pub. 1872, sheet 41.

1:2500 (25"): 2nd. edition, surveyed 1894–96, sheet LXXIII.

1:2500 (25"): 3rd edition, 1916, Greater London sheet IV.15.

1:1250 (50"): surveyed 1952, revised 1962, TQ2579NW & TQ2479NE.

Published sources

Addison, Joseph, 'Letters', *The Spectator*, April 1711 – September 1712.

Airs, Malcolm, 'Inigo Jones, Isaac de Caus and the Stables at Holland House', *The Georgian Group Journal*, vol. XIII, 2003.

Airs, Malcolm, 'Thorpe, John (1564/5–1655)', *Oxford Dictionary of National Biography*, Oxford University Press, Sept. 2004; online edn, Jan 2008.

Allen, Elizabeth, 'Cope, Sir Walter (1553?–1614)', *Oxford Dictionary of National Biography*, Oxford University Press, Sept. 2004; online edn, Jan 2008.

Barton, Nicholas, *The Lost Rivers of London*, Leicester University Press, 1962.

Blunt, Reginald (ed.), *Mrs Montagu 'Queen of the Blues' Her Letters and Friendships 1762–1800*, vol. 1, Constable & Co. Ltd., London, 1923.

Busse, John, *Mrs Montague, Queen of the Blues*, London, 1928.

Country Life, *Holland House, Kensington, a seat of the Earl of Ilchester*, vol xiii, 28 February 1903.

Dixon, Charles, *Catalogue of Plants growing in the gardens of Holland House, Kensington*, private printing, Hatchards, London, 1901.

Faulkner, Thomas, *History and Antiquities of Kensington*, London, 1820.

Fearnley-Whittingstall, Jane, *The Garden, An English Love Affair*, Weidenfeld & Nicholson, London, 2002.

Flood, Aidan, 'Nattes, John Claude (*c*.1765–1839)', *Oxford Dictionary of National Biography*, Oxford University Press, Sept 2004; online edn, May 2007.

Friends of Holland Park, *The Kyoto Garden in Holland Park*, 1991.

Friends of Holland Park and Royal Borough of Kensington & Chelsea Ecological Service, *Some Notable Trees of Holland Park, A Walk*, 2007.

Garnett, Richard, 'Rogers, Samuel (1763–1855)', Rev. Paul Baines, *Oxford Dictionary of National Biography*, Oxford University Press, 2004, online edn. May 2007.

Gloag, M. K., *A Book of English Gardens: Holland House*, Methuen, London, 1906.

Henderson, Paula, *The Tudor House and Garden*, Yale University Press, New Haven & London, 2005.

Hindle, Paul, *Maps for Historians*, Phillimore, Chichester, 1998.

Hobhouse, Penelope, *Plants in Garden History*, Pavilion, London, 1997.

Hudson, Derek, *Holland House in Kensington*, Peter Davies, London, 1967.

Ilchester, Countess of & Stavordale, Lord (eds), *The Life and Letters of Lady Sarah Lennox, 1745–1826*, John Murray, London, 1901.

Ilchester, Giles Stephen, 6th Earl of, *The Chronicles of Holland House, 1605–1820*, John Murray, London, 1937.

Ilchester, Giles Stephen, 6th Earl of, *The House of Holland, 1820–1900*, John Murray, London, 1937.

Jellicoe, Geoffrey & Susan; Goode, Patrick; Lancaster, Michael, *The Oxford Companion to Gardens*, Oxford University Press, 1986.

Langley, Batty, *New Principles of Gardening*, General Directions, VIII, 1728.

Liechtenstein, Princess Marie, *Holland House* (two vols.), Macmillan & Co., London, 1874.

Luff, Peter, 'Fox, Henry, first Baron Holland of Foxley (1705–1774)', *Oxford Dictionary of National Biography*, Oxford University Press, Sept 2004; online edn, Oct 2005.

Lysons, Daniel, *The Environs of London: Vol. 3: County of Middlesex*, 1795.

Martin, Trea, *Elizabeth in the Garden*, Faber & Faber, London, 2008.

Moffett, Cameron, 'A garden balustrade from Holland House', *English Heritage Historical review*, vol. 3, 2008, pp. 102–107.

Morris, Christopher (ed.), T*he Journeys of Celia Fiennes*, The Cresset Press, London, 1947.

Peck, Francis, *Desiderata Curiosa*, London, 1732–5.

Phibbs, John, 'The persistence of older traditions in eighteenth-century gardening'. *Garden History*, 37:2, winter 2009, pp. 174–188.

Pitman, Joanna, 'Some of London's Japanese gardens', *London Gardener*, vol. iv (1998–99), pp. 32–36.

Platter, Thomas & Busino, Horatio, *The Journals of Two Travellers in Elizabethan and Early Stewart England*, Caliban Books, London, 1995.

Plaw, John, *Ferme Ornée or Rural Improvements*, London, 1795.

Potter, Jennifer, *Strange Blooms, The Curious Lives and Adventures of the John Tradescants*, Atlantic Books, London, 2006.

Rogers, Pat, 'Addison, Joseph (1672–1719)', *Oxford Dictionary of National Biography*, Oxford University Press, Sept 2004; online edn, May 2009.

Rogers, Samuel, *Recollections 1763–1855* (ed. William Sharpe), London, 1859.

Smollett, Tobias, *Travels through France and Italy, 1766*, ed. Frank Felsenstein (Oxford, 1979), p. 263.

Smuts, Malcolm R., 'Rich, Henry, first Earl of Holland (bap. 1590, d. 1649)', *Oxford Dictionary of National Biography*, Oxford University Press, Sept 2004; online edn, May 2009.

Sorbière, Samuel de, *Voyage to England in 1652, containing many things relating to the state of Learning, Religion and other curiosities of that Kingdom 1652*, J. Woodward, London, 1708–9.

Starren, Carolyn, *The Families of Holland House*, London: Friends of Holland Park with Scotforth Books, 2012.

Survey of London: vol 37: Northern Kensington, 'The Holland Estate to 1874', 1973.

Symes Michael, *A Glossary of Garden History*, Shire Publications, Prices Risborough, 2000.

Symes, Michael, 'The Hon. Charles Hamilton at Holland Park', *Garden History*, vol. 3, no. 2, pp. 130–133.

The Gardener's Chronicle, vol. 25: 1899 and vol. 36, 1904.

Vincent, E. R. P., 'Some Italians at Holland House', MS. lecture, n.d. but post 1945, Royal Borough of Kensington & Chelsea Local Studies & Archive.

Wood, Christopher, *H is for Holland, The Sculptures and Architectural Features of Holland Park*, Friends of Holland Park.

Wroc, J. B., *Dahlias and their cultivation*, London, 1908.

Acknowledgements

The author and The Friends of Holland Park would like to acknowledge the generous assistance of the staff of Kensington and Chelsea Local Studies, which provided the majority of the illustrations.

THE ILLUSTRATIONS

Our grateful thanks go to the following for kindly allowing the reproduction of their images:

Front cover: By kind permission of The Royal Borough of Kensington & Chelsea Libraries.

Map of Holland Park: By kind permission of The Royal Borough of Kensington & Chelsea, reproduced by permission of Ordnance Survey on behalf of HMSO. © Crown copyright 2011. All rights reserved. Ordnance Survey Licence number 100053150.

Fig. 1, 49, 51: Reproduced by permission of English Heritage.NMR.

Fig. 2, 3, 5, 6, 7, 8, 12, 13, 14, 19, 20, 24, 26, 27, 28, 29, 31, 32, 33, 36, 37, 38, 58 & 60: By kind permission of The Royal Borough of Kensington & Chelsea Libraries.

Fig. 4: By courtesy of the Marquess of Salisbury.

Fig. 9: © National Portrait Gallery, London.

Fig. 10 & 11: By kind permission of Mr Mike Thrift.

Fig. 15, 16, 18, 21, 22, 23 & 25: © The Trustees of the British Museum.

Fig. 17: By kind permission of The Ilchester Estates.

Fig. 30: By kind permission of City of London, London Metropolitan Archives.

Fig. 34, 35, 39, 41, 43, 55, 57 & 59: By kind permission of Ordnance Survey.

Fig. 40, 46, 47, 48, 52, 53, 54 & 56: © *Country Life*.

Fig. 42: © RHS Lindley Library.

Fig. 44, 45 & 50: By kind permission of Sally Miller.

About the Author

Sally Miller studied for an MA in garden history from Birkbeck College, University of London in her retirement and is now a professional garden historian, who researches, writes and lectures on garden and landscape history. Having moved from London to Winchester, she contributes both to the work of the Hampshire Gardens Trust and the London Parks and Gardens Trust where she coordinates a group of volunteers who research material for www.londongardensonline.org.uk, a comprehensive database of the public parks, gardens, squares, historic greens and commons, cemeteries and churchyards of local historic interest in Greater London. She has previously published *The History of Bishops Park* and articles in *Garden History* and the *London Gardener*. Sally has family connections to Notting Hill from the 1940s and she lived there in the 1970s so Holland Park was a favourite place and she has enjoyed the opportunity, courtesy of The Friends of Holland Park, to explore its history.

The author wishes to thank garden historians Dr. Sally Jeffery and Dr. Paula Henderson for helpful and encouraging comments on the text while this book was being written, and William Charles (Bill) Noble for his expert analysis of Charles Dixon's catalogue of plants at Holland House.

The Friends of Holland Park

The Friends of Holland Park was founded in the early 1980s to secure the preservation, protection and improvement of Holland Park as a place of historic and ecological interest and beauty; to promote the conservation of the natural plant, animal and bird life of the Park and, in particular, its retention as a natural woodland habitat for wildlife; and to educate the public in the history, natural history and other aspects of the Park.

This publication was commissioned in pursuance of knowledge about the development over 350 years of 'the pleasure grounds' of Holland House by its illustrious owners until the great house was bombed during the Second World War.

For further details of the continuing work of The Friends and an invitation to join them, please see our website: www.thefriendsofhollandpark.org

Registered charity No. 281348